Out Of Town

Contents

Introduction

Out of Town is a collection of designs that feature SoHo and my cashmerino and alpaca silk ranges. Here is your capsule wardrobe for a rural retreat, snuggle into sweaters, longline tunics and jackets and enveloping coats. The designs showcase the yarns; a circular shawl style jacket relies on the drape of alpaca silk dk for the softness of its folds, the reversible fabric of cashmerino astrakhan is perfect for collared jackets, while the multi coloured effect of SoHo enlivens simple shapes. The patterns all feature larger sizes and include my favourite A line styles for a flattering silhouette.

Debbie Bliss

Basic Information

The quantities of yarn are based on average requirements and are therefore approximate. It is essential to work to the stated tension and you should always knit a tension square before starting. If you have too many stitches to 10cm/4in your tension is tight and you should change to a larger needle. If there are too few stitches, your tension is loose and you should change to a smaller needle. We cannot accept responsibility for the finished product if any yarn other than the one specified is used. Instructions given are for the first size, with larger sizes in round brackets. Where only one figure or instruction is given this applies to all sizes. Work all directions inside square brackets the number of times stated. See ball band for washing and pressing instructions.

STANDARD ABBREVIATIONS

alt = alternate
beg = beginning
cont = continue
dec = decrease
foll = following
inc = increase
k = knit
kfb = knit into front and back of st
m1 = make one st by picking up the loop lying between st just worked and next st and working into back of it
p = purl
pfb = purl into front and back of st
patt = pattern
psso = pass slipped st over
rem = remaining
rep = repeat
skpo = slip 1, knit 1, pass slipped stitch over
sl = slip
st(s) = stitch(es)
st st = stocking stitch
tbl = through back loop
tog = together
yf = yarn forward
yon = yarn over needle
yrn = yarn round needle

USA GLOSSARY

cast off = bind off
moss stitch = seed stitch
tension = gauge
stocking stitch = stockinette stitch
yarn forward, yarn over needle, or yarn round needle = yarn over

Classic Cabled Sweater

Double Breasted Jacket

Trapeze Jacket

Simple Coat

Slimline Jacket

Sweater Dress & Scarf

Flared Cable Jacket

Circular Cardigan

Smocked Cables Jacket

17

Shaped Edge Sweater

Patterns & schematics

Classic Cabled Sweater

MEASUREMENTS

To fit bust

81–86	92–97	102–107	cm
32–34	36–38	40–42	in

FINISHED MEASUREMENTS

Bust

94	104	114	cm
37	41	45	in

Length to shoulder

52	54	56	cm
20½	21¼	22	in

Sleeve length

46cm/18in for all sizes

MATERIALS

- 18(19:20) 50g balls of Debbie Bliss alpaca silk aran in Ginger 21.
- Pair each 4½mm (US 7) and 5mm (US 8) knitting needles.
- Cable needle.

TENSION

19 sts and 24 rows to 10cm/4in square over moss st using 5mm (US 8) needles.

ABBREVIATIONS

C2BW = slip next st onto cable needle and hold at back of work, p1, then p1 from cable needle.
C2FW = slip next st onto cable needle and hold at front of work, p1, then p1 from cable needle.
C3B = slip next st onto cable needle and hold at back of work, k2, then k1 from cable needle.
C3F = slip next 2 sts onto cable needle and hold at front of work, k1, then k2 from cable needle.
Cr3B = slip next st onto cable needle and hold at back of work, k2, then p1 from cable needle.
Cr3F = slip next 2 sts onto cable needle and hold at front of work, p1, then k2 from cable needle.
C5B = slip next 2 sts onto cable needle and hold at back of work, k3, then k2 from cable needle.
C6B = slip next 3 sts onto cable needle and hold at back of work, k3, then k3 from cable needle.
C6F = slip next 3 sts onto cable needle and hold at front of work, k3, then k3 from cable needle.
T2B = slip next st onto cable needle and hold at back of work, k1, then p1 from cable needle.
T2F = slip next st onto cable needle and hold at front of work, p1, then k1 from cable needle.
T4B = slip next 2 sts onto cable needle and hold at back of work, k2, then p2 from cable needle.
T4F = slip next 2 sts onto cable needle and hold at front of work, p2, then k2 from cable needle.
T4BP = slip next 2 sts onto cable needle and hold at back of work, k2, then [p1, k1] from cable needle.
T4FP = slip next 2 sts onto cable needle and hold at front of work, k1, p1, then k2 from cable needle.
dmst = double moss st.
Also see page 7.

PATTERN PANEL A (worked over 13 sts)

1st row (right side) P3, C3B, k1, C3F, p3.
2nd row K3, p3, k1, p3, k3.
3rd row P2, C3B, p1, k1, p1, C3F, p2.
4th row K2, p3, k1, p1, k1, p3, k2.
5th row P1, C3B, p1, [k1, p1] twice, C3F, p1.
6th row K1, p3, k1, [p1, k1] twice, p3, k1.
7th row C3B, p1, [k1, p1] 3 times, C3F.
8th row P3, k1, [p1, k1] 3 times, p3.
9th row K2, p1, [k1, p1] 4 times, k2.
10th row P2, k1, [p1, k1] 4 times, p2.
11th row Cr3F, p1, [k1, p1] 3 times, Cr3B.
12th row K1, p2, k1, [p1, k1] 3 times, p2, k1.
13th row P1, Cr3F, p1, [k1, p1] twice, Cr3B, p1.
14th row K2, p2, k1, [p1, k1] twice, p2, k2.
15th row P2, Cr3F, p1, k1, p1, Cr3B, p2.

16th row K3, p2, k1, p1, k1, p2, k3.
17th row P3, Cr3F, p1, Cr3B, p3.
18th row K4, p2, k1, p2, k4.
19th row P4, C5B, p4.
20th row K4, p5, k4.
These 20 rows form patt panel A and are repeated throughout.

PATTERN PANEL B (worked over 12 sts)

1st row (right side) [K1, p1] 4 times, T4B.
2nd row K1, p3, [k1, p1] 4 times.
3rd row [k1, p1] 3 times, T4B, T2F.
4th row P1, k2, p3, [k1, p1] 3 times.
5th row [K1, p1] twice, T4B, T2F, T2B.
6th row K1, C2BW, k2, p3, [k1, p1] twice.
7th row K1, p1, T4B, T2F, T2B, T2F.
8th row P1, k2, C2FW, k2, p3, k1, p1.
9th row T4B, [T2F, T2B] twice.
10th row K1, C2BW, k2, C2BW, k2, p3.
11th row T4FP, [T2B, T2F] twice.
12th row As 8th row.
13th row K1, p1, T4FP, T2B, T2F, T2B.
14th row As 6th row.
15th row [K1, p1] twice, T4FP, T2B, T2F.
16th row As 4th row.
17th row [K1, p1] 3 times, T4FP, T2B.
18th row As 2nd row.
19th row [K1, p1] 4 times, T4FP.
20th row P2, [k1, p1] 5 times.
These 20 rows form patt panel B and are repeated throughout.

PATTERN PANEL C (worked over 12 sts)

1st row (right side) T4F, [p1, k1] 4 times.
2nd row [P1, k1] 4 times, p3, k1.
3rd row T2B, T4F, [p1, k1] 3 times.
4th row [P1, k1] 3 times, p3, k2, p1.
5th row T2F, T2B, T4F, [p1, k1] twice.
6th row [P1, k1] twice, p3, k2, C2FW, k1.
7th row T2B, T2F, T2B, T4F, p1, k1.
8th row P1, k1, p3, k2, C2BW, k2, p1.
9th row [T2F, T2B] twice, T4F.
10th row P2, k3, C2FW, k2, C2FW, k1.
11th row [T2B, T2F] twice, T4BP.
12th row As 8th row.
13th row T2F, T2B, T2F, T4BP, p1, k1.
14th row As 6th row.
15th row T2B, T2F, T4BP, [p1, k1] twice.
16th row As 4th row.
17th row T2F, T4BP, [p1, k1] 3 times.
18th row As 2nd row.
19th row T4BP, [p1, k1] 4 times.
20th row [P1, k1] 5 times, p2 .
These 20 rows form patt panel C and are repeated throughout.

BACK

With 4½ mm (US 7) needles cast on 101(109:121) sts.
1st rib row (right side) K1, * p1, k1; rep from * to end.
2nd rib row P1, * k1, p1; rep from * to end.
Rep the last 2 rows until rib measures 10cm/4in from cast on edge, ending with a 1st rib row.
Inc row Rib 27(31:37), m1, rib 3, m1, rib 19, m1, rib 3, m1, rib 19, m1, rib 3, m1, rib 27(31:37). 107(115:127) sts.
Change to 5mm (US 8) needles and work in patt as follows:
1st row (right side) [K1, p1] 4(6:9) times, p2, work across 1st row of panel A, p2, k3, C6F, p2, work across 1st row of panel B, p1, k3, C6F, p1, work across 1st row of panel C, p2, k3, C6F, p2, work across 1st row of panel A, p2, [p1, k1] 4(6:9) times.
2nd row [P1, k1] 4(6:9) times, k2, work across 2nd row of panel A, k2, p9, k2, work across 2nd row of panel C, k1, p9, k1, work across 2nd row of panel B, k2, p9, k2, work across 2nd row of panel A, k2, [k1, p1] 4(6:9) times.
3rd row [P1, k1] 4(6:9) times, p2, work across 3rd row of panel A, p2, C6B, k3, p2, work across 3rd row of panel B, p1, C6B, k3, p1, work across 3rd row of panel C, p2, C6B, k3, p2, work across 3rd row of panel A, p2, [k1, p1] 4(6:9) times.
4th row [K1, p1] 4(6:9) times, k2, work across 4th row of panel A, k2, p9, k2, work across 4th row of panel C, k1, p9, k1, work across 4th row of panel B, k2, p9, k2, work across 4th row of panel A, k2, [p1, k1] 4(6:9) times.
These 4 rows **set** the position for the patt panels and **form** the cable panels and moss st.
Cont in patt until work measures 13cm/5in from cast on edge, ending with a wrong side row.
Change to 4½ mm (US 7) needles.
Cont in patt until work measures 21(22:23)cm/8¼(8¾:9)in from cast on edge, ending with a wrong side row.
Change to 5mm (US 8) needles.
Cont in patt until work measures 33(34:35)cm/13(13½:13¾)in from cast on edge, ending with a wrong side row.
Shape armholes
Cast off 8(10:12) sts at beg of next 2 rows. 91(95:103) sts. **
Cont straight until work measures 52(54:56)cm/20½(21¼:22)in from cast on edge, ending with a wrong side row.
Shape shoulders
Cast off 14(15:16) sts at beg of next 2 rows and 15(15:17) sts at beg of foll 2 rows.
Leave rem 33(35:37) sts on a spare needle.

FRONT

Work as given for Back to **.
Cont straight in patt until front measures 47(49:51)cm/18½(19¼:20)in from cast on edge, ending with a wrong side row.
Shape neck
Next row Patt 34(35:38), turn and work on these sts for first side of neck shaping.

Dec one st at neck edge on next 5 rows. 29(30:33) sts.
Work straight until front matches Back to shoulder shaping ending at armhole edge.

Shape shoulder
Cast off 14(15:16) sts at beg of next row.
Work 1 row.
Cast off rem 15(15:17) sts.
With right side facing slip centre 23(25:27) sts onto a holder, join on yarn, patt to end.
Complete to match first side, reversing shapings.

SLEEVES

With 4½ mm (US 7) needles cast on 55 sts.
1st rib row (wrong side) P1, * k1, p1; rep from * to end.
2nd rib row K1, * p1, k1; rep from * to end.
Rep the last 2 rows until rib measures 10cm/4in from cast on edge, ending with a 1st rib row.
Inc row (wrong side) Rib 4, m1, rib 3, m1, rib 19, m1, rib 3, m1, rib 19, m1, rib 3, m1, rib 4. 61 sts.
Change to 5mm (US 8) needles and work in patt as follows:
1st row (right side) P2, k3, C6F, p2, work across 1st row of panel B, p1, k3, C6F, p1, work across 1st row of panel C, p2, k3, C6F, p2.
2nd row K2, p9, k2, work across 2nd row of panel C, k1, p9, k1, work across 2nd row of panel B, k2, p9, k2.
3rd row P2, C6B, k3, p2, work across 3rd row of panel B, p1, C6B, k3, p1, work across 3rd row of panel C, p2, C6B, k3, p2.
4th row K2, p9, k2, work across 4th row of panel C, k1, p9, k1, work across 4th row of panel B, k2, p9, k2.
These 4 rows **set** the position for the patt panels and **form** the cable panels.
Inc and work into dmst one st at each end of the next row and every foll 4th row until there are 65(83:101) sts, then on 14(7:0) foll 5th rows. 93(97:101) sts.
Cont straight until sleeve measures 46cm/18in from cast on edge, ending with a wrong side row.
Mark each end of last row with a coloured thread.
Work a further 6(8:10) rows.

Shape sleeve top
Cast off 8(7:6) sts at beg of next 10(12:14) rows.
Cast off rem 13(13:17) sts.

COLLAR

Join right shoulder seam.
With right side facing and 4½ mm (US 7) needles, pick up and k16 sts down left side of front neck, k across 23(25:27) sts at centre front, pick up and k16 sts up right side of front neck, k across 33(35:37) sts at back neck. 88(92:96) sts.
Rib row * K1, p1; rep from * to end.
Rep this row for 10cm/4in.
Change to 5mm (US 8) needles.
Cont in rib until collar measures 24cm/9½ in.
Cast off loosely in rib.

TO MAKE UP

Join left shoulder seam and collar, reversing seam on last 14cm/5½ in of collar. Sew sleeves into armholes with row ends above markers sewn to sts cast off at underarm. Join side and sleeve seams.

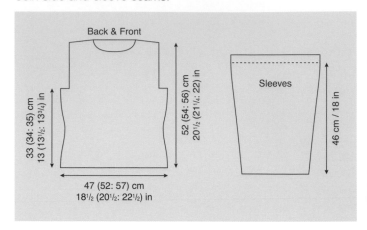

Deep V Sweater

MEASUREMENTS

To fit bust

86–91	97–102	107–112	cm
34–36	38–40	42–44	in

FINISHED MEASUREMENTS

Bust

112	120	128	cm
44	47¼	50½	in

Length

66	68	70	cm
26	26¾	27½	in

Sleeve length

46cm/18in for all sizes

MATERIALS

- 19(20:21) 50g balls of Debbie Bliss SoHo in Spice 17.
- Pair each 3¾ mm (US 5) and 5mm (US 8) knitting needles.
- 3¾ mm (US 5) circular needle.
- Cable needle.

TENSION

20 sts and 21 rows to 10cm/4in square over trellis patt using 5mm (US 8) needles.

ABBREVIATIONS

C2L = slip first st onto cable needle, hold at front, k1, then k1 from cable needle.
C2LP = slip first st onto cable needle, hold at front, p1, then k1 from cable needle.
C2R = k into front of 2nd st, then into front of first st, slip both sts off left needle together.
C2RP = k into front of 2nd st, p 2nd st, slip both sts off left needle together.
m1k = make one st by picking up and knitting into back of yarn lying between st just worked and next st.
m1p = make one st by picking up and purling into back of yarn lying between st just worked and next st.
Also see page 7.

TRELLIS PATTERN

1st row (wrong side) K1, p1, [k2, p2] to last 4 sts, k2, p1, k1.
2nd row P1, [C2LP, C2RP] to last st, p1.
3rd row K2, [p2, k2] to end.
4th row P2, [C2R, p2] to end.
5th row As 3rd row.
6th row P1, [C2RP, C2LP] to last st, p1.
7th row As 1st row.
8th row P1, k1, [p2, C2L] to last 4 sts, p2, k1, p1.
These 8 rows form the trellis patt and are repeated.

BACK

With 3¾ mm (US 5) needles, cast on 106(114:122) sts.
1st row (right side) K2, [p2, k2] to end.
2nd row P2, [k2, p2] to end.
These 2 rows form rib.
Rib 16 more rows.
P 1 row.
Change to 5mm (US 8) needles and work 13 rows in trellis patt.
1st inc row (right side) P1, m1k, patt to last st, m1k, p1. 108(116:124) sts.
Patt 1 row.
2nd inc row P1, m1p, patt to last st, m1p, p1. 110(118:126) sts.
Patt 17 rows.
Work first inc row, next row and 2nd inc row again. 114(122:130) sts **.
Patt 41 rows.
Shape armholes
Next row (right side) Cast off 6 sts, patt to last 6 sts, cast off 6 sts.

With wrong side facing, rejoin yarn to rem 102(110:118) sts and work as follows:
Dec row (wrong side) K2tog, patt to last 2 sts, skpo. 100(108:116) sts.
Cont in patt, dec in this way at each end of next 7(9:11) wrong side rows. 86(90:94) sts.
Patt 31 rows, so ending with a right side row.
Cast off.
Place markers, 18 sts in from each end of cast off row.

FRONT

Work as given for Back to **.
Patt 15 rows.
Shape neck and armholes
Next row (right side) Patt 57(61:65), turn and cont on these sts only, leave rem sts on a spare needle.
Dec row (wrong side) K2tog, patt to end. 56(60:64) sts.
Cont in patt, dec in this way at beg of next 12 wrong side rows. 44(48:52) sts.
Next row (right side) Cast off 6 sts, patt to end. 38(42:46) sts.
*** **Dec row** (wrong side) K2tog, patt to last 2 sts, skpo.
Patt 1 row.
Rep the last 2 rows until 22 sts rem, ending with a right side row.
Next row (wrong side) K2tog, patt to end.
Patt 1 row.
Rep the last 2 rows twice more and the dec row again. 18 sts.
Patt 23 rows, so ending with a right side row.
Cast off ***.
With right side facing, rejoin yarn to rem 57(61:65) sts and patt to end.
Dec row (wrong side) Patt to last 2 sts, skpo.
Cont in patt, dec in this way at end of next 12 wrong side rows. 44(48:52) sts.
Next row (right side) Patt to last 6 sts, cast off 6 sts.
With wrong side facing, rejoin yarn to rem 38(42:46) sts and work as first side of neck from *** to ***.

SLEEVES

With 3¾mm (US 5) needles, cast on 58(62:66) sts.
Rib 18 rows as given for Back.
P 1 row.
Change to 5mm (US 8) needles.
Work 13 rows in trellis patt.
1st inc row (right side) P1, m1k, patt to last st, m1k, p1. 60(64:68) sts.
Patt 1 row.
2nd inc row P1, m1p, patt to last st, m1p, p1. 62(66:70) sts.
Patt 9 rows.
Rep the last 12 rows 5 times more. 82(86:90) sts.
Shape top Cast off 6 sts at beg and at end of next row.
With wrong side facing, rejoin yarn to rem 70(74:78) sts

and and work as follows:
Dec row (wrong side) K2tog, patt to last 2 sts, skpo. 68(72:76) sts.
Cont in patt, dec in this way at each end of next 7(9:11) wrong side rows. 54 sts.
Cast off loosely.

COLLAR

Join shoulder seams using back neck markers as a guide.
With 3¾mm (US 5) circular needle, pick up and k 75(79:83) sts up right front neck, 50(54:58) sts across back neck and 75(79:83) sts down left front neck. 200(212:224) sts.
K 1 row.
1st row (right side) K3, [p2, k2] to last st, k1.
2nd row P3, [k2, p2] to last st, p1.
These 2 rows form rib with one extra st at each end and are repeated.
Rib 19 more rows.
Cast off knitwise.

TO MAKE UP

Sew sleeves into armholes. Join side and sleeve seams.
Overlap ends of collar and slipstitch row ends to neck edge.

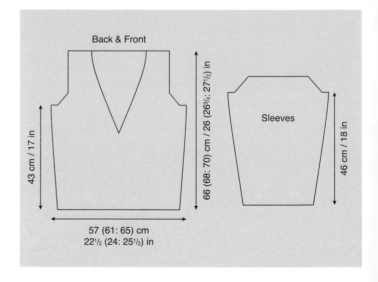

Back & Front

43 cm / 17 in

66 (68: 70) cm / 26 (26¾: 27½) in

57 (61: 65) cm
22½ (24: 25½) in

Sleeves

46 cm / 18 in

Double Breasted Jacket

MEASUREMENTS

To fit bust

81–86	91–97	102–107	cm
32–34	36–38	40–42	in

FINISHED MEASUREMENTS

Bust

96	107	118	cm
37¾	42	46½	in

Length to shoulder

47	51	55	cm
18½	20	21¾	in

Sleeve length

43	46	48	cm
17	18	19	in

MATERIALS

- 19(21:23) 50g balls of Debbie Bliss alpaca silk aran in Claret 24.
- Pair each 4mm (US 6), 4½mm (US 7), 5mm (US 8) and 5½mm (US 9) knitting needles.
- 8 buttons.

TENSION

18 sts and 24 rows to 10cm/4in square over double moss st using 5mm (US 8) needles.

ABBREVIATIONS

See page 7.

BACK

With 4mm (US 6) needles cast on 89(99:109) sts.
Work in patt as follows:
1st row (right side) K1, * p1, k1; rep from * to end.
2nd row P1, * k1, p1; rep from * to end.
3rd row P1, * k1, p1; rep from * to end.
4th row K1, * p1, k1; rep from * to end.
These 4 rows form the double moss st patt and are repeated throughout.
Cont in patt until work measures 8cm/3in from cast on edge, ending with a wrong side row.
Change to 4½ mm (US 7) needles.
Cont in patt until work measures 16(17:18)cm/6¼(6¾:7)in from cast on edge, ending with a wrong side row.
Change to 5mm (US 8) needles.
Cont in patt until work measures 28(30:32)cm/11(11¾:12½)in from cast on edge, ending with a wrong side row.
Shape armholes
Cast off 8(9:10) sts at beg of next 2 rows. 73(81:89) sts.
Cont straight until work measures 47(51:55)cm/18½(20:21¾)in from cast on edge, ending with a wrong side row.
Shape shoulders
Cast off 11(12:14) sts at beg of next 2 rows and 11(13:14) sts at beg of foll 2 rows.
Cast off rem 29(31:33) sts.

LEFT FRONT

With 4mm (US 6) needles cast on 59(65:71) sts.
Work in patt as follows:
1st row (right side) P1, * k1, p1; rep from * to end.
2nd row K1, * p1, k1; rep from * to end.
3rd row K1, * p1, k1; rep from * to end.
4th row P1, * k1, p1; rep from * to end.
These 4 rows form the double moss st patt and are repeated throughout.
Cont in patt until work measures 8cm/3in from cast on edge, ending with a wrong side row.
Change to 4½ mm (US 7) needles.
Cont in patt until work measures 16(17:18)cm/6¼(6¾:7)in from cast on edge, ending with a wrong side row.
Change to 5mm (US 8) needles.
Cont in patt until work measures 28(30:32)cm/11(11¾:12½)in from cast on edge, ending with a wrong side row.
Shape armhole
Cast off 8(9:10) sts at beg of next row. 51(56:61) sts.
Next row Patt to end.

Next row With 5mm (US 8) needles, patt 22(25:28), with 5½ mm (US 9) needles, patt 29(31:33).
Next row With 5½ mm (US 9) needles, patt 29(31:33), with 5mm (US 8) needles, patt 22(25:28).
Rep these 2 rows until front measures same as Back to shoulder, ending at armhole edge.

Shape shoulder
Cast off 11(12:14) sts at beg of next row and 11(13:14) sts at beg of foll alt row. 29(31:33) sts.

Collar
Next row With 4mm (US 6) needles, patt 8(9:10), with 5½ mm (US 9) needles, patt 21(22:23).
Next row With 5½ mm (US 9) needles, patt 21(22:23), with 4mm (US 6) needles, patt 8(9:10).
Rep the last 2 rows until short edge (edge nearest the shoulder) of collar measures 10(10:11)cm/4(4:4¼)in,
Cast off in patt.
Mark position for buttons, the first pair on the 5th row from cast on edge, the fourth pair, 23(25:27)cm/9(10:10¾)in from cast on edge, with the remaining two pairs spaced evenly between.

RIGHT FRONT

With 4mm (US 6) needles cast on 59(65:71) sts.
Work in patt as follows:
1st row (right side) P1, * k1, p1; rep from * to end.
2nd row K1, * p1, k1; rep from * to end.
3rd row K1, * p1, k1; rep from * to end.
4th row P1, * k1, p1; rep from * to end.
These 4 rows form the double moss st patt and are repeated throughout.
Buttonhole row (right side) [P1, k1] twice, yf, k2tog, patt 19(21:23), k2tog, yf, patt to end.
The remaining buttonholes are worked in the same way in positions to match markers.
Cont in patt until work measures 8cm/3in from cast on edge, ending with a wrong side row.
Change to 4½mm (US 7) needles.
Cont in patt until work measures 16(17:18)cm/6¼(6¾:7)in from cast on edge, ending with a wrong side row.
Change to 5mm (US 8) needles.
Cont in patt until work measures 28(30:32)cm/11(11¾:12½)in from cast on edge, ending with a right side row.

Shape armhole
Cast off 8(9:10) sts at beg of next row. 51(56:61) sts.
Next row With 5½mm (US 9) needles, patt 29(31:33), with 5mm (US 8) needles, patt 22(25:28).
Next row With 5mm (US 8) needles, patt 22(25:28), with 5½mm (US 9) needles, patt 29(31:33).
Rep these 2 rows until front measures same as Back to shoulder, ending at armhole edge.

Shape shoulder
Cast off 11(12:14) sts at beg of next row and 11(13:14) sts at beg of foll alt row. 29(31:33) sts.

Collar
Next row With 5½ mm (US 9) needles, patt 21(22:23), with 4mm (US 6) needles, patt 8(9:10).
Next row With 4mm (US 6) needles, patt 8(9:10), with 5½ mm (US 9) needles, patt 21(22:23).
Rep the last 2 rows until short edge of collar measures 10(10:11)cm/4(4:4¼)in.
Cast off in patt.

SLEEVES

With 4½ mm (US 7) needles, cast on 43(47:51) sts.
Work in patt as follows:
1st row (right side) K1, * p1, k1; rep from * to end.
2nd row P1, * k1, p1; rep from * to end.
3rd row P1, * k1, p1; rep from * to end.
4th row K1, * p1, k1; rep from * to end.
These 4 rows form the double moss st patt and are repeated throughout.
Work a further 12 rows.
Change to 5mm (US 8) needles.
Inc and work into patt, one st at each end of 3rd and every foll 6th row until there are 69(75:81) sts.
Cont straight until sleeve measures 43(46:48)cm/17(18:19)in from cast on edge, ending with a wrong side row.
Place markers at each end of last row.
Work a further 10(10:12) rows.
Cast off.

TO MAKE UP

Join shoulder seams. Sew sleeves into armholes with row ends above markers sewn to sts cast off at underarm. Join side and sleeve seams. Join cast off edges of collar. Sew row ends of collar to back neck edge. Sew on buttons.

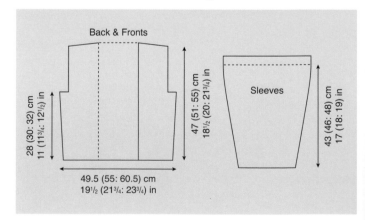

Trapeze Jacket

MEASUREMENTS

To fit bust

86	92	97	102	107	112	cm
34	36	38	40	42	44	in

FINISHED MEASUREMENTS

Bust

97.5	102	106.5	111	115	120	cm
38½	40¼	42	43¾	45¼	47¼	in

Length

72	73	74	74.5	75.5	76	cm
28¼	28¾	29¼	29½	29¾	30	in

Sleeve (before turning back cuff)

50 cm/19¾ in for all sizes

MATERIALS

- 20(21:22:23:24:25:26) 50g balls of Debbie Bliss alpaca silk aran in Purple 25.
- Pair each of 4½ mm (US 7) and 5mm (US 8) knitting needles.
- 4 buttons.

TENSION

18 sts and 24 rows to 10cm/4in square over st st using 5mm (US 8) needles.

ABBREVIATIONS

s2kpo = slip next 2 sts as if to k2tog, k1, pass slipped sts over.
Also see page 7.

BACK

With 4½ mm (US 7) needles, cast on 138(142:146:150:154:158) sts.
K 2 rows.
Change to 5mm (US 8) needles.
1st row (right side) K14(15:16:17:18:19), * p2, k13, p2, k10, p2, k13, p2 *, k22(24:26:28:30:32); rep from * to *, k14(15:16:17:18:19).
2nd row P14(15:16:17:18:19), * k2, p13, k2, p10, k2, p13, k2 *, p22(24:26:28:30:32); rep from * to *, p14(15:16:17:18:19).
These 2 rows form panels of st st with p2 ribs between.
Work 6 more rows.
1st dec row (right side) K14(15:16:17:18:19), * p2, k1, k2tog, k7, skpo, k1, p2, k10, p2, k1, k2tog, k7, skpo, k1, p2 *, k22(24:26:28:30:32); rep from * to *, k14(15:16:17:18:19). 130(134:138:142:146:150) sts.
Work 19 rows.
2nd dec row (right side) K14(15:16:17:18:19), * p2, k1, k2tog, k5, skpo, k1, p2, k10, p2, k1, k2tog, k5, skpo, k1, p2 *, k22(24:26:28:30:32); rep from * to *, k14(15:16:17:18:19). 122(126:130:134:138:142) sts.
Work 17 rows.
3rd dec row (right side) K14(15:16:17:18:19), * p2, k1, k2tog, k3, skpo, k1, p2, k10, p2, k1, k2tog, k3, skpo, k1, p2 *, k22(24:26:28:30:32); rep from * to *, k14(15:16:17:18:19). 114(118:122:126:130:134) sts.
Work 15 rows.
4th dec row (right side) K14(15:16:17:18:19), * p2, k1, k2tog, k1, skpo, k1, p2, k10, p2, k1, k2tog, k1, skpo, k1, p2 *, k22(24:26:28:30:32); rep from * to *, k14(15:16:17:18:19). 106(110:114:118:122:126) sts.
Work 13 rows.
5th dec row (right side) K14(15:16:17:18:19), * p2, k1, s2kpo, k1, p2, k10, p2, k1, s2kpo, k1, p2 *, k22(24:26:28:30:32); rep from * to *, k14(15:16:17:18:19). 98(102:106:110:114:118) sts.
Work 11 rows.
6th dec row (right side) K14(15:16:17:18:19), * p2, s2kpo, p2, k10, p2, s2kpo, p2 *, k22(24:26:28:30:32); rep from * to *, k14(15:16:17:18:19). 90(94:98:102:106:110) sts.
Work 29 rows.
Shape armholes
Cast off 4(4:5:5:6:6) sts at beg of next 2 rows.
82(86:88:92:94:98) sts.

Dec row (right side) K3, k2tog, patt to last 5 sts, skpo, k3. 80(84:86:90:92:96) sts.
Dec in this way at each end of next 5(6:6:7:7:8) right side rows. 70(72:74:76:78:80) sts.
Work 39(39:41:41:43:43) rows without shaping.
Cast off.
Place markers 15(16:17:18:19:20) sts in from each end of cast off row.

LEFT FRONT

With 4½ mm (US 7) needles, cast on 72(74:76:78:80:82) sts.
K 2 rows.
Change to 5mm (US 8) needles.
1st row (right side) K14(15:16:17:18:19), p2, k13, p2, k10, p2, k13, p2, k14(15:16:17:18:19).
2nd row P14(15:16:17:18:19), k2, p13, k2, p10, k2, p13, k2, p14(15:16:17:18:19).
These 2 rows form panels of st st with p2 ribs between.
Work 6 more rows.
1st dec row (right side) K14(15:16:17:18:19), p2, k1, k2tog, k7, skpo, k1, p2, k10, p2, k1, k2tog, k7, skpo, k1, p2, k14(15:16:17:18:19). 68(70:72:74:76:78) sts.
Work 19 rows.
2nd dec row (right side) K14(15:16:17:18:19), p2, k1, k2tog, k5, skpo, k1, p2, k10, p2, k1, k2tog, k5, skpo, k1, p2, k14(15:16:17:18:19). 64(66:68:70:72:74) sts.
Work 17 rows.
3rd dec row (right side) K14(15:16:17:18:19), p2, k1, k2tog, k3, skpo, k1, p2, k10, p2, k1, k2tog, k3, skpo, k1, p2, k14(15:16:17:18:19). 60(62:64:66:68:70) sts.
Work 15 rows.
4th dec row (right side) K14(15:16:17:18:19), p2, k1, k2tog, k1, skpo, k1, p2, k10, p2, k1, k2tog, k1, skpo, k1, p2, k14(15:16:17:18:19). 56(60:62:64:66:68) sts.
Work 13 rows.
5th dec row (right side) K14(15:16:17:18:19), p2, k1, s2kpo, k1, p2, k10, p2, k1, s2kpo, k1, p2, k14(15:16:17:18:19). 52(54:56:58:60:62) sts.
Work 11 rows.
6th dec row (right side) K14(15:16:17:18:19), p2, s2kpo, p2, k10, p2, s2kpo, p2, k14(15:16:17:18:19). 48(50:52:54:56:58) sts.
Work 29 rows **.
Shape armhole
Cast off 4(4:5:5:6:6) sts at beg of next row. 44(46:47:49:50:52) sts.
Work 1 row.
Dec row (right side) K3, k2tog, patt to end. 43(45:46:48:49:51) sts.
Cont in patt and dec in this way at beg of next 5(6:6:7:7:8) right side rows. 38(39:40:41:42:43) sts.
Work 15(15:17:17:19:19) rows.

Shape neck
Next row (right side) Patt 26(27:28:29:30:31), turn and leave rem 12 sts on a holder for neck.
Dec one st at neck edge on next 11 rows. 15(16:17:18:19:20) sts.
Patt 12 rows.
Cast off.
Place markers for buttons, the top one on the last right side row before neck shaping with 3 more spaced 24 rows apart.

RIGHT FRONT

Buttonhole row (right side) K1, skpo, yo twice, k2tog, patt to end.
On next row, p into back of first yo and p into front of 2nd yo.
Work as given for Left Front to **, working buttonholes to match markers, as given.
Patt 1 more row.
Shape armhole
Next row (wrong side) Cast off 4(4:5:5:6:6) sts, patt to end. 44(46:47:49:50:52) sts.
Dec row (right side) Patt to last 5 sts, skpo, k3. 43(45:46:48:49:51) sts.
Cont in patt and dec in this way at end of next 5(6:6:7:7:8) right side rows. 38(39:40:41:42:43) sts.
Work 15(15:17:17:19:19) rows.
Shape neck
Next row (right side) K12 and leave these 12 sts on a holder for neck, patt to end.
Dec one st at neck edge on next 11 rows. 15(16:17:18:19:20) sts.
Patt 12 rows.
Cast off.

SLEEVES

With 4½ mm (US 7) needles, cast on 50(50:52:52:54:54) sts.
K 2 rows.
Change to 5mm (US 8) needles.
Beg with a k row, work 24(24:20:24:24:14) rows in st st.
Inc row (right side) K1, kfb, k to last 3 sts, kfb, k2. 52(52:54:54:56:56) sts.
Taking all inc sts into st st, inc in this way at each end of 9(11:12:14:15:17) foll 10th(8th:8th:6th:6th:6th) rows. 70(74:78:82:86:90) sts.
Work 3(5:1:9:3:1) rows in st st.
Shape top
Cast off 4(4:5:5:6:6) sts at beg of next 2 rows. 62(66:68:72:74:78) sts.
Dec row (right side) K1, k2tog, k to last 3 sts, skpo, k1. 60(64:66:70:72:76) sts.
Cont in st st and dec in this way at each end of next 7(9:9:11:11:13) right side rows. 46(46:48:48:50:50) sts.
P 1 row.
Cast off.

NECKBAND

Join shoulder seams, using markers on back neck edge
as a guide.
With 4½ mm (US 7) needles, slip 12 sts from right front holder
onto needle, pick up and k18 sts up right front neck,
31(32:33:34:35:36) sts across back neck and 18 sts down
left front neck then k12 from left front holder.
91(92:93:94:95:96) sts.
K 2 rows.
Cast off knitwise.

FRONT EDGINGS

With 4½ mm (US 7) needles and omitting neckband, pick up
and k 100(102:104:106:108:110) sts up right front edge.
K 2 rows.
Cast off knitwise.
Work Left Front edging in the same way.

TO MAKE UP

Sew sleeves into armholes. Join side and sleeve seams,
reversing seam for turn-back cuff. Join ends of neckband
and front edgings. Sew on buttons.

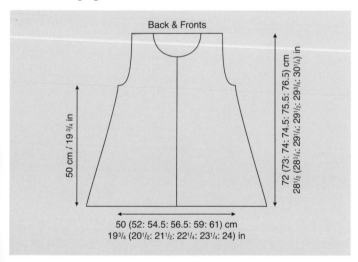

Back & Fronts

72 (73: 74: 74.5: 75.5: 76.5) cm
28½ (28¾: 29¼: 29½: 29¾: 30¼) in

50 cm / 19 ¾ in

50 (52: 54.5: 56.5: 59: 61) cm
19¾ (20½: 21½: 22¼: 23¼: 24) in

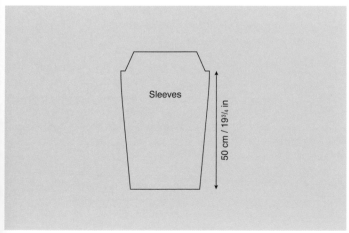

Sleeves

50 cm / 19¾ in

Simple Coat

MEASUREMENTS

To fit bust

86–92	97–102	107–112	cm
34–36	38–40	42–44	in

FINISHED MEASUREMENTS

Bust

104	113	122	cm
41	44½	48	in

Length to shoulder

72	75	78	cm
28¼	29½	30¾	in

Sleeve length

46	48	50	cm
18	19	19¾	in

MATERIALS

- 16(18:19) 50g balls of Debbie Bliss cashmerino astrakhan in Damson 21.
- Pair each size 4mm (US 6) and 4½ mm (US 7) knitting needles.

TENSION

18 sts and 26 rows to 10cm/4in square over st st using 4½ mm (US 7) needles.

ABBREVIATIONS

See page 7.

BACK

With 4mm (US 6) needles, cast on 116(124:132) sts.
K 3 rows.
Change to 4½ mm (US 7) needles.
Beg with a k row, work 10 rows in st st.
Dec row (right side) K5, skpo, k to last 7 sts, k2tog, k5.
Work 11 rows in st st.
Rep the last 12 rows 8 times more and then the dec row once again. 96(104:112) sts.
Cont straight until back measures 51(53:55)cm/ 20(20¾:21¾)in from cast on edge, ending with a p row.
Shape armholes
Cast off 9 sts at beg of next 2 rows. 78(86:94) sts.
Cont straight until back measures 72(75:78)cm/ 28¼(29½:30¾)in from cast on edge, ending with a p row.
Shape shoulders
Cast off 11(12:14) sts loosely at beg of next 2 rows, then 11(13:14) sts at beg of foll 2 rows.
Leave rem 34(36:38) sts on a holder.

LEFT FRONT

With 4mm (US 6) needles, cast on 74(80:86) sts.
K 3 rows.
Change to 4½ mm (US 7) needles.
Next row (right side) K.
Next row K3, p to end.
These 2 rows form st st with garter st front edge and are repeated.
Work 8 rows.
Dec row (right side) K5, skpo, k to end.
Work 11 rows.
Rep the last 12 rows 8 times more, then the dec row once again. 64(70:76) sts.
Cont straight until front matches Back to armhole, ending with a wrong side row.
Shape armhole
Next row (right side) Cast off 9 sts, k to end. 55(61:67) sts.
Cont straight in patt until front measures 67(70:73)cm/ 26½(27½:28¾)in from cast on edge, ending with a k row.
Shape neck
Next row (wrong side) K33(36:39), p to end.
K 1 row.
Rep the last 2 rows once more.
Next row Cast off 33(36:39) sts knitwise, p to end.
22(25:28) sts
Cont straight until front matches Back to shoulder, ending

with a p row.

Shape shoulder

Next row Cast off 11(12:14) sts loosely, k to end.

P 1 row.

Next row Cast off rem 11(13:14) sts loosely.

RIGHT FRONT

With 4mm (US 6) needles, cast on 74(80:86) sts.

K 3 rows.

Change to 4½mm (US 7) needles.

Next row (right side) K.

Next row P to last 3 sts, k3.

These 2 rows form st st with garter st front edge and
are repeated.

Work 8 rows.

Dec row (right side) K to last 7 sts, k2tog, k5.

Work 11 rows.

Rep the last 12 rows 8 times more, then the dec row
once again. 64(70:76) sts.

Cont straight until front matches Back to armhole,
ending with a k row.

Shape armhole

Next row (wrong side) Cast off 9 sts, p to last 3 sts, k3.
55(61:67) sts.

Cont straight in patt until front measures 67(70:73)cm/
26½(27½:28¾)in from cast on edge, ending with a k row.

Shape neck

Next row P to last 33(36:39) sts, k to end.

Next row K.

Rep the first of these 2 rows once more, so ending with
a wrong side row.

Next row Cast off 33(36:39) sts, k to end. 22(25:28) sts.

Cont straight until front matches Back to shoulder, ending
with a k row.

Shape shoulder

Next row Cast off 11(12:14) sts loosely, p to end.

K 1 row.

Next row Cast off rem 11(13:14) sts loosely.

SLEEVES

With 4mm (US 6) needles, cast on 38(40:42) sts.

K 3 rows.

Change to 4½mm (US 7) needles.

Beg with a k row, work 10 rows in st st.

1st inc row (right side) K2, m1, k to last 2 sts, m1, k2.

Work 4 rows.

2nd inc row (wrong side) P2, m1, p to last 2 sts, m1, p2.

Work 4 rows.

Cont in this way to inc 1 st at each end of next row
and every foll 5th row until there are 76(80:84) sts.

Cont straight until sleeve measures 46(48:50)cm/
18(19:19¾)in from cast on edge.

Mark each end of last row.

Work a further 12 rows.

Cast off loosely.

COLLAR

Join shoulder seams. Place markers on front neck cast off
edge, 10cm/4in in from front edge.

With wrong side of jacket facing and 4½mm (US 7) needles,
pick up and k 27(29:31) sts along left front neck edge from
marker to shoulder, k across 34(36:38) sts on back neck
holder, then pick up and k27(29:31) sts down right front
neck edge from shoulder to marker. 88(94:100) sts.

K 3 rows.

4th row (right side of collar) K3, p to last 3 sts, k3.

Next 2 rows K to last 15 sts, turn, sl 1, p to last 15 sts, turn.

Next 2 rows Sl 1, k to last 20 sts, turn, sl 1, p to last
20 sts, turn.

Next 2 rows Sl 1, k to last 25 sts, turn, sl 1, p to last
25 sts, turn.

Next 2 rows Sl 1, k to last 30 sts, turn, sl 1, p to last
30 sts, turn.

Next 2 rows Sl 1, k to last 35 sts, turn, sl 1, p to last
35 sts, turn.

Next row K to end.

Next row K3, p to last 3 sts, k3.

Rep the last 2 rows for a further 7cm/2 3/4in, ending
with a k row.

K 4 rows.

Cast off knitwise loosely.

TO MAKE UP

With centre of cast off edge of sleeve to shoulder, sew
sleeves into armholes. Join side and sleeve seams.

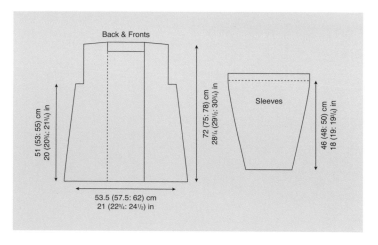

Slimline Jacket

MEASUREMENTS

To fit bust

86	92	97	102	107	cm
34	36	38	40	42	in

FINISHED MEASUREMENTS

Bust

91	95	100	104	108	cm
35¾	37½	39½	41	42½	in

Length to shoulder

55	57	59	61	63	cm
21¾	22½	23¼	24	24¾	in

Sleeve length

45	45	45	46	46	cm
17¾	17¾	17¾	18	18	in

MATERIALS

- 9(10:11:12:13) 50g balls of Debbie Bliss cashmerino astrakhan in Lilac 20.
- Pair of 4½ mm (US 7) knitting needles.
- 2 buttons.

TENSION

18 sts and 26 rows to 10cm/4in square over st st using 4½mm (US 7) needles.

ABBREVIATIONS

See page 7.

BACK

With 4½ mm (US 7) needles, cast on 84(88:92:96:100) sts.
K 1 row.
Beg with a k row, work in st st.
Work 16 rows.
Dec row K5, skpo, k to last 7 sts, k2tog, k5.
Work 3 rows.
Rep the last 4 rows 4 times more and the dec row again.
72(76:80:84:88) sts.
Work 13(15:17:19:21) rows.
Inc row K3, m1, k to last 3 sts, m1, k3.
Work 5 rows.
Rep the last 6 rows until there are 84(88:92:96:100) sts.
Cont straight until back measures 35(36:37:38:39)cm/
13¾(14¼:14½:15:15¼)in from cast on edge, ending with a p row.
Shape armholes
Cast off 6(6:7:7:8) sts at beg of next 2 rows.
72(76:78:82:84) sts.
Dec one st at each end of next row and every foll right side row until 60(62:64:66:68) sts rem.
Cont straight in st st until back measures 55(57:59:61:63)cm/21¾(22½:23¼:24:24¾)in from cast on edge, ending with a p row.
Shape shoulders
Cast off 8(8:8:9:9) sts at beg of next 2 rows and 8(9:9:9:9) sts at beg of foll 2 rows.
Cast off rem 28(28:30:30:32) sts.

LEFT FRONT

With 4½mm (US 7) needles, cast on 45(47:49:51:53) sts.
K 1 row.
Next row (right side) K to end.
Next row K2, p to end.
These 2 rows form st st with garter st front edge and are repeated.
Work 14 rows.
Dec row K5, skpo, k to end.
Work 3 rows.
Rep the last 4 rows 4 times more and the dec row again.
39(41:43:45:47) sts.
Work 13(15:17:19:21) rows.
Inc row K3, m1, k to end.
Work 5 rows.
Rep the last 6 rows 4 times more and the inc row again.
45(47:49:51:53) sts.

Cont straight until front measures 35(36:37:38:39)cm/
13¾(14¼:14½:15:15¼)in from cast on edge, ending
at side edge with a wrong side row.

Shape armhole

Next row Cast off 6(6:7:7:8) sts, k to end.
39(41:42:44:45) sts.

Next row K2, p to end.

Next row Skpo, k to end.
Rep the last 2 rows 5(6:6:7:7) times more.
33(34:35:36:37) sts.
Cont straight until front measures 50(52:54:56:58)cm/
19¾(20½:21¼:22:22¾)in, ending at front edge.

Shape neck

Next row (wrong side) K17(17:18:18:19), p to end.
K 1 row.
Rep the last 2 rows once more.

Next row Cast off 17(17:18:18:19) sts, p to end.
Cont on rem 16(17:17:18:18) sts until front measures
same as Back to shoulder, ending at armhole edge.

Shape shoulder

Cast off 8(8:8:9:9) sts at beg of next row.
P 1 row.
Cast off rem 8(9:9:9:9) sts.
Place a marker on neck cast off edge, 3cm/1¼in in from
front edge.
Mark position for two buttons, the first 21(22:23:24:25)cm/
8¼(8¾:9:9½:9¾)in from cast on edge and the second,
10cm/4in above.

RIGHT FRONT

Work buttonholes to match button positions as follows:
1st buttonhole row (right side) K2, k2tog, [yrn] twice,
skpo, k to end.
2nd buttonhole row P to last 2 sts, working
[p1, p1 tbl] into double yrn of previous row, k2.
With 4½ mm (US 7) needles, cast on 45(47:49:51:53) sts.
K 1 row.

Next row (right side) K to end.

Next row P to last 2 sts, k2.
These 2 rows form st st with garter st front edge
and are repeated.
Work 14 rows.

Dec row K to last 7 sts, k2tog, k5.
Work 3 rows.
Rep the last 4 rows 4 times more and the dec row again.
39(41:43:45:47) sts.
Work 13(15:17:19:21) rows.

Inc row K to last 3 sts, m1, k3.
Work 5 rows.
Working buttonholes to match markers, rep the last 6 rows 4
times more and the inc row again. 45(47:49:51:53) sts.
Cont straight until front measures 35(36:37:38:39)cm/
13¾(14¼:14½:15:15¼)in from cast on edge, ending at side
edge with a right side row.

Shape armhole

Next row Cast off 6(6:7:7:8) sts, p to last 2 sts, k2.
39(41:42:44:45) sts.

Next row K to last 2 sts, k2tog.

Next row P to last 2 sts, k2.
Rep the last 2 rows 5(6:6:7:7) times more.
33(34:35:36:37) sts.
Cont straight until front measures 50(52:54:56:58)cm/
19¾(20½:21¼:22:22¾)in, ending at side edge.

Shape neck

Next row (wrong side) P to last 17(17:18:18:19) sts, k to end.
K 1 row.

Next row P to last 17(17:18:18:19) sts, k to end.

Next row Cast off 17(17:18:18:19) sts, k to end.
Cont on rem 16(17:17:18:18) sts until front measures
same as Back to shoulder, ending at armhole edge.

Shape shoulder

Cast off 8(8:8:9:9) sts, at beg of next row.
K 1 row.
Cast off rem 8(9:9:9:9) sts.
Place a marker on neck cast off edge, 3cm/1¼in in from
front edge.

SLEEVES

With 4½ mm (US 7) needles cast on 34(38:42:46:50) sts.
K 1 row.
Beg with a k row, work in st st.
Work 12 rows.

Inc row K3, m1, k to last 3 sts, m1, k3.
Work 7 rows.
Rep the last 8 rows until there are 56(60:64:68:72) sts.
Cont straight until sleeve measures 45(45:45:46:46)cm/
17¾(17¾:17¾:18:18)in from cast on edge, ending
with a p row.

Shape sleeve top

Cast off 6(6:7:7:8) sts st beg of next 2 rows.
44(48:50:54:56) sts.
Dec 1 st at each end of the next row and every foll 4th row
until 38(38:40:40:42) sts rem, then on every foll alt row until
20(20:22:22:24) sts rem.
Work 1 row.
Cast off 3 sts at beg of next 2 rows.
Cast off rem 14(14:16:16:18) sts.

COLLAR

Join shoulder seams.
With wrong side of jacket facing and 4½ mm (US 7) needles,
pick up and k 21 sts from left front marker to shoulder seam,
28 sts across back neck edge and 21 sts across right front
from shoulder to marker. 70 sts.

1st row (wrong side of collar) K3, p to last 3 sts, k3.
2nd row K.
3rd row K3, p to last 3 sts, k3.
Next 2 rows K to last 6 sts, turn, sl 1, p to last 6 sts, turn.

Next 2 rows K to last 10 sts, turn, sl 1, p to last 10 sts, turn.
Next 2 rows K to last 14 sts, turn, sl 1, p to last 14 sts, turn.
Next 2 rows K to last 18 sts, turn, sl 1, p to last 18 sts, turn.
Next 2 rows K to last 22 sts, turn, sl 1, p to last 22 sts, turn.
Next row K across all sts.
Next row K3, p to last 3 sts, k3.
Rep the last 2 rows until collar measures 5cm/2in from pick
up edge, measured at the row ends, and ending with
a wrong side row.
K 3 rows.
Cast off purlwise.

TO MAKE UP

Sew sleeves into armholes. Join side and sleeve seams.
Sew on buttons.

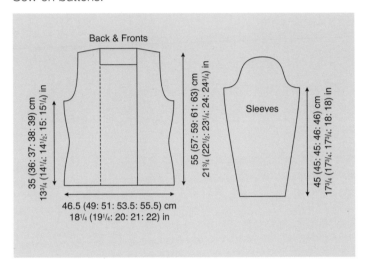

Sweater Dress

MEASUREMENTS

To fit bust

86–91	97–102	107–112	cm
34–36	38 40	42–44	in

FINISHED MEASUREMENTS

Bust

102	111	120	cm
40	43¾	47¼	in

Length

73	76	79	cm
28¾	30	31	in

Sleeve length

44	46	48	cm
17¼	18	19	in

MATERIALS

- 17(19:21) 50g balls of Debbie Bliss alpaca silk dk in Flax 14.
- Pair each 3¾ mm (US 5) and 4mm (US 6) knitting needles
- 3¾ mm (US 5) circular needle.
- Cable needle.

TENSION

26 sts and 32 rows to 10cm/4in square over double moss st using 4mm (US 6) needles.

ABBREVIATIONS

C5B = slip next 2 sts onto cable needle, hold at back of work, k3, then p1, k1tbl from cable needle.
C5F = slip next 3 sts onto cable needle, hold at front of work, k1tbl, p1, then k3 from cable needle.
C6B = slip next 3 sts onto cable needle, hold at back of work, k3, then k3 from cable needle.
C6F = slip next 3 sts onto cable needle, hold at front of work, k3, then k3 from cable needle.
C7B = slip next 4 sts onto cable needle, hold at back of work, k3, return end st from cable needle to left needle, hold cable needle to front of work, p1, then k3 from cable needle.
dmst = double moss st.
Also see page 7.

CHEVRON PANEL (Worked over 25 sts)

1st row (right side) P9, k3, p1, k3, p9.
2nd and every wrong side row K and p the sts as they appear.
3rd row As 1st row.
5th row P9, C7B, p9.
7th row P7, C5B, p1, C5F, p7.
9th row P7, k3, [p1, k1tbl] twice, p1, k3, p7.
11th row P5, C5B, [p1, k1tbl] twice, p1, C5F, p5.
13th row P5, k3, [p1, k1tbl] 4 times, p1, k3, p5.
15th row P3, C5B, [p1, k1tbl] 4 times, p1, C5F, p3.
17th row P3, k3, [p1, k1tbl] 6 times, p1, k3, p3.
19th row P1, C5B, [p1, k1tbl] 6 times, p1, C5F, p1.
21st row P1, k3, [p1, k1tbl] 8 times, p1, k3, p1.
23rd row P25.
24th row K25.
These 24 rows form the chevron patt panel and are repeated.

BACK

With 3¾ mm (US 5) needles, cast on 153(165:177) sts.
1st row (right side) K3, [p3, k3] to end.
2nd row P3, [k3, p3] to end.
These 2 rows form rib.
Rib 48 more rows.
Dec row (right side) Rib 39(45:51), p3tog, [rib 33, p3tog] twice, rib 39(45:51). 147(159:171) sts.
Next row K.
Change to 4mm (US 6) needles.
1st row (right side) [K1, p1] 9(12:15) times, [k9, work 25 sts of 1st row of chevron patt panel] 3 times, k9, [p1, k1] 9(12:15) times.
2nd and every wrong side row K and p the sts as they appear.
3rd row [P1, k1] 8(11:14) times, p2, [C6B, k3, work 25 sts of 3rd row of chevron patt panel] twice, k3, C6F, work 25 sts of 3rd row of chevron patt panel, k3, C6F, p2, [k1, p1] 8(11:14) times.
5th row As 1st but working 25 sts of 5th row of chevron patt panel each time.

7th row [P1, k1] 8(11:14) times, p2, [k3, C6F, work 25 sts of 7th row of chevron patt panel] twice, C6B, k3, work 25 sts of 7th row of chevron panel, C6B, k3, p2, [k1, p1] 8(11:14) times.
8th row As 2nd row.
These 8 rows **form** plait cables between and at each side of 3 chevron patt panels with double moss st to each side. Cont in patt as set and work 38 more rows, working correct chevron patt panel rows.
Inc row (right side) Kfb, patt to last 2 sts, kfb, k1. 149(161:173) sts.
Taking inc sts into double moss st, cont in patt and inc in this way at each end of 4 foll 10th rows. 157(169:181) sts.
Patt 37 rows.
Shape armholes
Cast off 10 sts at beg of next 2 rows. 137(149:161) sts.
Dec row (right side) P2tog, patt to last 2 sts, p2tog. 135(147:159) sts.
Cont in patt, dec in this way at each end of next 11(13:15) right side rows. 113(121:129) sts **.
Patt 31(35:41) rows straight.
Cast off.
Place markers 31(35:39) sts in from each end of cast off row.

FRONT

Work as given for Back to **.
Patt 15(19:25) rows, so ending with 20th(4th:14th) row of 7th(8th:8th) repeat of chevron panels.
Shape neck
Next row (right side) Patt 44(48:52), turn and complete left side on these sts.
[Cast off 2 sts at beg of next row and dec one st at end of foll row] 4 times.
Patt 1 row.
Dec one st at end of next row. 31(35:39) sts.
Patt 5 rows.
Cast off.
With right side facing, slip centre 25 sts onto a holder, rejoin yarn to rem 44(48:52) sts, patt to end.
[Dec one st at end of next row and cast off 2 sts at beg of foll row] 4 times.
Patt 1 row.
Dec one st at beg of next row. 31(35:39) sts.
Patt 5 rows.
Cast off.

SLEEVES

With 3¾ mm (US 5) needles, cast on 69(81:81) sts.
Work 28 rows in rib as given for Back.
Dec row (right side) Rib 33(39:39), p3tog, rib 33(39:39). 67(79:79) sts.
Next row K.
Change to 4mm (US 6) needles.
1st row (right side) [K1, p1] 6(9:9) times, k9, work 25 sts of 1st row of chevron patt panel, k9, [p1, k1] 6(9:9) times.

2nd and every wrong side row K and p the sts as they appear.
3rd row [P1, k1] 5(8:8) times, p2, C6B, k3, work 25 sts of 3rd row of chevron patt panel, k3, C6F, p2, [k1, p1] 5(8:8) times.
5th row As 1st row but working 25 sts of 5th row of chevron panel.
7th row [P1, k1] 5(8:8) times, p2, k3, C6F, work 25 sts of 7th row of chevron panel, C6B, k3, p2, [k1, p1] 5(8:8) times.
8th row As 2nd row.
These 8 rows **form** plait cables and double moss st at each side of chevron panel.
Cont in patt as set working correct patt panel rows and work 26(32:2) more rows.
Inc row (right side) Kfb, patt to last 2 sts, kfb, k1.
Taking incs into double moss st, cont in patt, inc in this way at each end of 11(11:17) foll 6th rows. 91(103:115) sts.
Patt 9 rows.
Shape top
Cast off 10 sts at beg of next 2 rows. 71(83:95) sts.
Next row (right side) P2tog, patt to last 2 sts, p2tog.
Patt 1 row.
Rep the last 2 rows 11(13:15) times more. 47(55:63) sts.
Cast off 2 sts at beg and dec one st at end of next 4(6:8) rows. 35(37:39) sts.
Cast off.

COLLAR

Join shoulder seams, using back edge markers as a guide. With 3¾ mm (US 5) circular needle, pick up and k45 sts across back neck edge and 21 sts down left front neck then work across sts on centre front holder as follows: **1st size** m1, p1, m1, k2, skpo, [k1tbl, p1] 7 times, k1tbl, k2tog, k2, m1, p1, m1; **2nd size** m1, p8, k2tog, k2, m1, p1, m1, k2, skpo, p8, m1; **3rd size** k3, C5F, m1, [p1, k1tbl] 4 times, p1, m1, C5F, k3; then for **all sizes**, pick up and k21 sts up right front neck. 114 sts.
1st round P.
2nd round [P3, k3] to end.
2nd round forms rib and is repeated.
Cont in rib until collar measures 17cm/6¾ in.
Cast off in rib.

TO MAKE UP

Sew sleeves into armholes. Taking 1½ sts into seams to match rib, join side and sleeve seams.

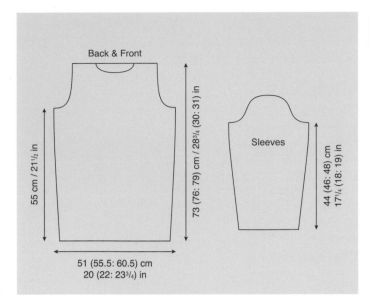

Back & Front

55 cm / 21½ in

73 (76: 79) cm / 28¾ (30: 31) in

51 (55.5: 60.5) cm
20 (22: 23¾) in

Sleeves

44 (46: 48) cm
17¼ (18: 19) in

Striped scarf

SIZE

Approximately 14 x 214cm/5½ x 84in.

MATERIALS

- Two 50gm balls of Debbie Bliss cashmerino chunky in each of Grey 20 (A) and Rust 16 (B)
- Pair 7mm (US 10½–11) knitting needles.

TENSION

15½ sts and 17 rows to 10cm/4in square over patt when lightly pressed, using 7mm (US 10½–11) needles.

ABBREVIATIONS

See page 7.

NOTE

This scarf uses all of the stated yarn. Avoid leaving too long ends when changing colours or you will need to break into a 3rd ball of each shade.

TO MAKE

With 7mm (US 11) needles and A, cast on 22sts.
1st row Knit.
2nd row K2, [p3, k2] to end.
These 2 rows form the patt and are repeated throughout.
Work a further 24 rows.
Change to B and work 26 rows in pattern.
Rep the last 52 rows 6 times more.
Cast off.

Flared Cable Jacket

MEASUREMENTS

To fit bust

81–86	91–97	102–107	cm
32–34	36–38	40–42	in

FINISHED MEASUREMENTS

Bust

88	99	110	cm
34¾	39	43¼	in

Length

73	75	77	cm
28¾	29½	30¼	in

Sleeve length

45cm/17¾ in for all sizes

MATERIALS

- 15(17:19) 50g balls of Debbie Bliss cashmerino aran in Burnt Orange 15.
- Pair of 5mm (US 8) knitting needles.
- 4¼mm (US 7) and 5mm (US 8) circular needles.
- Cable needle.
- 4 buttons.

TENSION

20 sts and 26 rows to 10cm/4in square over double moss st (dmst) using 5mm (US 8) needles.

ABBREVIATIONS

C4BP = slip next st onto cable needle, hold at back of work, k3, then p1 from cable needle.
C4FP = slip next 3 sts onto cable needle, hold at front of work, p1, then k3 from cable needle.
C6B = slip next 3 sts onto cable needle, hold at back of work, k3, then k3 from cable needle.
C6F = slip next 3 sts onto cable needle, hold at front of work, k3, then k3 from cable needle.
dmst = double moss st.
Also see page 7.

NOTES

- The cable band is worked first. Stitches are picked up along the left edge to work the lower part in one piece with increases in the 6 cable panels to give a flared shape. Stitches are then picked up along the right edge to work the top in double moss stitch.
- When picking up stitches for the lower part, pick up one stitch from every row of the cable band for the first size, omit two rows for the 2nd size and pick up one stitch from the cast on and cast off edges as well as one stitch from every row for the 3rd size.
- When picking up stitches for the upper part, place markers to divide the cable band into 4 and pick up 40(46:52) sts from first section, 40(45:50) sts from the 2nd section, one extra st at centre back and 40(45:50) sts from 3rd section and 40(46:52) sts from 4th section.

PATTERN PANEL A (Worked over 10 sts on the first row, increasing to 18 sts)

1st and 3rd rows (right side) P2, k6, p2.
2nd row K2, p6, k2.
4th row M1, k2, p6, k2, m1. 12 sts.
5th row P3, C6B, p3.
6th and every wrong side row except for 12th, 24th and 40th rows K and p the sts as they appear.
7th row P2, C4BP, C4FP, p2.
9th row P2, [k3, p2] twice.
11th row P2, C4FP, C4BP, p2.
12th row M1, k3, p6, k3, m1. 14 sts.
13th row P4, C6B, p4.
15th row P3, C4BP, C4FP, p3.
17th row P2, C4BP, p2, C4FP, p2.
19th row P2, k3, p4, k3, p2.
21st row P2, C4FP, p2, C4BP, p2.
23rd row P3, C4FP, C4BP, p3.
24th row M1, k4, p6, k4, m1. 16 sts.
25th row P5, C6B, p5.

27th row P4, C4BP, C4FP, p4.
29th row P3, C4BP, p2, C4FP, p3.
31st row P2, C4BP, p4, C4FP, p2.
33rd row P2, k3, p6, k3, p2.
35th row P2, C4FP, p4, C4BP, p2.
37th row P3, C4FP, p2, C4BP, p3.
39th row P4, C4FP, C4BP, p4.
40th row M1, k5, p6, k5, m1. 18 sts.
41st row P6, C6B, p6.
43rd row P5, C4BP, C4FP, p5.
45th row P4, C4BP, p2, C4FP, p4.
47th row P3, C4BP, p4, C4FP, p3.
49th row P2, C4BP, p6, C4FP, p2.
51st row P2, k3, p8, k3, p2.
53rd row P2, C4FP, p6, C4BP, p2.
55th row P3, C4FP, p4, C4BP, p3.
57th row P4, C4FP, p2, C4BP, p4.
59th row P5, C4FP, C4BP, p5.
60th row K6, p6, k6.
These 60 rows form Patt Panel A.

PATTERN PANEL B

Work as given for Patt Panel A but work C6F instead of C6B on 5th, 13th, 25th and 41st rows.

PATTERN PANEL C (Worked over 16 sts)

1st row (right side) K1tbl, p4, k6, p4, k1tbl.
2nd row P1tbl, k4, p6, k4, p1tbl.
3rd row K1tbl, p4, k6, p4, k1tbl.
4th row P1tbl, k4, p6, k4, p1tbl.
5th row (right side) K1tbl, p4, C6F, p4, k1tbl.
6th and every wrong side row K and p the sts as they appear, working tbl sts of previous row as p1tbl.
7th row K1tbl, p3, C4BP, C4FP, p3, k1tbl.
9th row K1tbl, p2, C4BP, p2, C4FP, p2, k1tbl.
11th row K1tbl, p2, k3, p4, k3, p2, k1tbl.
13th row K1tbl, p2, C4FP, p2, C4BP, p2, k1tbl.
15th row K1tbl, p3, C4FP, C4BP, p3, k1tbl.
16th row See 6th row.
These 16 rows form Patt Panel C, 1st to 4th rows are worked once and 5th to 16th rows only are repeated.

PATTERN PANEL D

As Patt Panel C but working C6B instead of C6F on 5th row.

CABLE BAND

With 5mm (US 8) needles, cast on 8 sts.
1st row (right side) P1, k6, p1.
2nd row K1, p6, k1.
3rd and 4th rows As 1st and 2nd rows.
5th row P1, C6B, p1.
6th row As 2nd row.
These 6 rows form the cable band patt and are repeated.

Work 205(223:235) more rows, so ending with 1st row of 36th(39th:41st) repeat. 211(229:241) rows in total have been completed.
Cast off knitwise.

FRONTS AND BACK

(Worked in one piece to armholes)
Lower part (Skirt)
With right side facing and 4½ mm (US 7) circular needle, pick up and k 211(227:243) sts from row-ends of left edge of cable band (see Notes).
Change to 5mm (US 8) circular needle and work in rows not rounds.
K 1 row.
Work in patt as follows:
1st row (right side) P1, [k1, p1] 7(8:9) times, k1tbl, work 10 sts of 1st row of Patt Panel A, k1tbl, * p1, [k1, p1] 9(10:11) times, k1tbl, work 10 sts of 1st row of Patt Panel A, k1tbl, rep from * once, p1, [k1, p1] 16(18:20) times, ** k1tbl, work 10 sts of 1st row of Patt Panel B, k1tbl, p1, [k1, p1] 9(10:11) times, rep from ** once, k1tbl, work 10 sts of 1st row of Patt Panel B, k1tbl, p1, [k1, p1] 7(8:9) times.
2nd row K1, [p1, k1] 7(8:9) times, p1tbl, work 2nd row of Patt Panel B, p1tbl, * k1, [p1, k1] 9(10:11) times, p1tbl, work 2nd row of Patt Panel B, p1tbl, rep from * once, k1, [p1, k1] 16(18:20) times, ** p1tbl, work 2nd row of Patt Panel A, p1tbl, k1, [p1, k1] 9(10:11) times, rep from ** once, p1tbl, work 2nd row of Patt Panel A, p1tbl, k1, [p1, k1] 7(8:9) times.
3rd row K1, [p1, k1] 7(8:9) times, k1tbl, work 3rd row of Patt Panel A, k1tbl, * k1, [p1, k1] 9(10:11) times, k1tbl, work 3rd row of Patt Panel A, k1tbl, rep from * once, k1, [p1, k1] 16(18:20) times, ** k1tbl, work 3rd row of Patt Panel B, k1tbl, k1, [p1, k1] 9(10:11) times, rep from ** once, k1tbl, work 3rd row of Patt Panel B, k1tbl, k1, [p1, k1] 7(8:9) times.
4th row P1, [k1, p1] 7(8:9) times, p1tbl, work 4th row of Patt Panel B, p1tbl, * p1, [k1, p1] 9(10:11) times, p1tbl, work 4th row of Patt Panel B, p1tbl, rep from * once, p1, [k1, p1] 16(18:20) times, ** p1tbl, work 4th row of Patt Panel A, p1tbl, p1, [k1, p1] 9(10:11) times, rep from ** once, p1tbl, work 4th row of Patt Panel A, p1tbl, p1, [k1, p1] 7(8:9) times.
223(239:255) sts.
These 4 rows **set** the position of 6 cable panels with dmst outlined with tbl sts between and at each side. Remembering that on right side rows the first 3 panels are panel A with C6B and the last 3 panels are panel B with C6F.
Work in patt, increasing as given for panels A and B on 12th, 24th and 40th rows. 259(275:291) sts.
Cont in patt and rep 41st to 60th rows of panels twice more, then work 41st and 42nd rows again.
Next row (right side) Dmst 16(18:20), [p5, k2tog, k4, skpo, p5, dmst 21(23:25)] 3 times, dmst 14(16:18), [p5, k2tog, k4, skpo, p5, dmst 21(23:25)] twice, p5, k2tog, k4, skpo, p5, dmst 16(18:20). 247(263:279) sts.
K2 rows.
Cast off knitwise.

Upper part (Yoke)

With right side facing and 4½ mm (US 7) circular needle, pick up and k 161(183:205) sts from row-ends of right edge of cable band. (See Notes)

K 1 row.

Change to 5mm (US 8) circular needle and work in patt as follows:

1st row (right side) P1, [k1, p1] 19(22:25) times, k1tbl, p1, [k1, p1] 40(45:50) times, k1tbl, p1, [k1, p1] 19(22:25) times.

2nd row K1, [p1, k1] 19(22:25) times, p1tbl, k1, [p1, k1] 40(45:50) times, p1tbl, k1, [p1, k1] 19(22:25) times.

3rd row K1, [p1, k1] 19(22:25) times, k1tbl, k1, [p1, k1] 40(45:50) times, k1tbl, k1, [p1, k1] 19(22:25) times.

4th row P1, [k1, p1] 19(22:25) times, p1tbl, p1, [k1, p1] 40(45:50) times, p1tbl, p1, [k1, p1] 19(22:25) times.

These 4 rows **form** dmst with tbl sts as mock side seams.

1st inc row (right side) Dmst 39(45:51), m1, k1tbl, m1, dmst 81(91:101), m1, k1tbl, m1, dmst 39(45:51). 165(187:209) sts.

Taking incs into dmst, work 5 rows.

2nd inc row Dmst 40(46:52), m1, k1tbl, m1, dmst 83(93:103), m1, k1tbl, m1, dmst 40(46:52). 169(191:213) sts.

Taking incs into dmst, work 5 rows.

3rd inc row Dmst 41(47:53), m1, k1tbl, m1, dmst 85(95:105), m1, k1tbl, m1, dmst 41(47:53). 173(195:217) sts.

Cont in dmst with tbl sts for mock seams, work 14 rows, so ending with a right side row.

Divide for underarms

Next row (wrong side) Dmst 39(45:51), cast off 7 sts for left underarm, dmst until there are 81(91:101) sts on right needle after cast off sts, cast off 7 sts for right underarm, dmst to end.

Right front

Work on first 39(45:51) sts and leave rem groups of sts on holders for back and left front.

Dec row (right side) Dmst to last 2 sts, skpo. 38(44:50) sts.

Cont in dmst, dec in this way at end of next 3(5:7) right side rows. 35(39:43) sts.

Work 11(13:15) rows in dmst.

Cut yarn.

Shape neck

Next row (right side) Slip first 14(15:16) sts onto a holder for neck, rejoin yarn to rem 21(24:27) sts, dmst to end.

Dmst 1 row.

Dec row (right side) K2tog, dmst to end. 20(23:26) sts.

Cont in dmst, dec in this way at beg of next 4 right side rows. 16(19:22) sts.

Work 24 rows in dmst, so ending with a right side row.

Cast off.

Back

With right side facing, work on centre 81(91:101) sts.

Dec row (right side) K2tog, dmst to last 2 sts, skpo. 79(89:99) sts.

Cont in dmst, dec in this way at each end of next 3(5:7) right side rows. 73(79:85) sts.

Work 16(18:50) rows in dmst, so ending with a right side row.

Cast off.

Place markers 16(19:22) sts in from each end of cast off row of back.

Left front

With right side facing, work on last 39(45:51) sts.

Dec row (right side) K2tog, dmst to end. 38(44:50) sts.

Cont in dmst, dec in this way at beg of next 3(5:7) right side rows. 35(39:43) sts.

Work 11(13:15) rows in dmst.

Shape neck

Next row (right side) Dmst to last 14(15:16) sts, turn and leave last 14(15:16) sts on a holder for neck. 21(24:27) sts.

Dmst 1 row.

Dec row (right side) Dmst to last 2 sts, skpo. 20(23:26) sts.

Cont in dmst, dec in this way at end of next 4 right side rows. 16(19:22) sts.

Work 24 rows in dmst, so ending with a right side row.

Cast off.

SLEEVES

Left sleeve

With 5mm (US 8) needles, cast on 50(54:58) sts.

K 2 rows.

Work in patt as follows:

1st row (right side) P1, [k1, p1] 8(9:10) times, work 16 sts of 1st row Patt Panel C, p1, [k1, p1] 8(9:10) times.

2nd row K1, [p1, k1] 8(9:10) times, work 16 sts of 2nd row Patt Panel C, k1, [p1, k1] 8(9:10) times.

3rd row K1, [p1, k1] 8(9:10) times, work 16 sts of 3rd row Patt Panel C, k1, [p1, k1] 8(9:10) times.

4th row P1, [k1, p1] 8(9:10) times, work 16 sts of 4th row Patt Panel C, p1, [k1, p1] 8(9:10) times.

These 4 rows **set** the position for the cable panel and **form** dmst at each side.

5th row Dmst 17(19:21), work 16 sts of 5th row of Patt Panel C, dmst 17(19:21).

Cont in patt, working repeats of 5th to 16th rows of Patt Panel C.

Work 3 more rows.

Inc row (right side) P1, m1, patt to last st, m1, p1. 52(56:60) sts.

Taking inc sts into dmst, inc in this way at each end of 13(15:17) foll 8th(6th:6th) rows. 78(86:94) sts.

Patt 7(21:9) rows.

Shape top

Cast off 4 sts at beg of next 2 rows. 70(78:86) sts.

Dec row P2tog, patt to last 2 sts, p2tog. 68(76:84) sts.

Cont in patt, dec in this way at each end of next 7(9:11) right side rows. 54(58:62) sts.

Patt 1 row.

Cast off.

Right sleeve

Work as Left Sleeve but working Panel D for Panel C.

NECKBAND

Join shoulder seams using back edge markers as a guide. With 4½ mm (US 7) circular needle, work 14(15:16) sts in dmst from right front holder, pick up and k 25(26:28) sts up right front neck, 41(43:43) sts across back neck and 25(26:28) sts down left front neck, dmst 14(15:16) from holder. 119(125:131) sts.

1st row K.
2nd row (right side) K4, [p3, k3] to last st, k1.
3rd row P4, [k3, p3] to last st, p1.
2nd and 3rd rows form rib.
Rib 3 more rows.
Cast off knitwise.

BUTTONHOLE BAND

With right side facing and 4½ mm (US 7) needles, pick up and k 82 sts up lower right front to cable band, 6 sts from band and 43(49:55) sts along upper right front to neck. 131(137:143) sts.

1st row K.
2nd row K4, [p3, k3] to last st, k1.
3rd row K1, p3, [k3, p3] to last st, k1.
2nd and 3rd rows form rib with k1 at each end.
Buttonhole row (right side) Rib 83(84:84), yo, p2tog(k2tog:k2tog), rib 13(14:16), yo, k2tog(p2tog, k2tog), rib 13(14:16), yo, p2tog(k2tog:k2tog), rib 13(14:16), yo, k2tog, k1(3:3).
Rib 4 more rows.
Cast off knitwise.

BUTTON BAND

With right side of left front facing and 4½ mm (US 7) needles, pick up and k 43(49:55) down upper left front from neck to cable band, 6 sts from band and 82 sts down lower left front to cast off edge. 131(137:143) sts.
Work to match Buttonhole Band, omitting buttonholes.

TO MAKE UP

Join sleeve seams. Sew sleeves into armholes.
Sew on buttons.

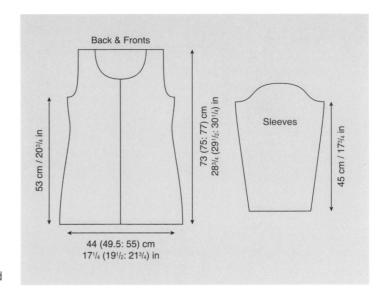

Circular Cardigan

MEASUREMENTS

To fit bust

81–86	91–97	102–107	cm
32–34	36–38	40 –42	in

FINISHED MEASUREMENTS

Bust and Length
(across circle excluding pointed edging)

87	106	123	cm
34¼	41¾	48½	in

Sleeve length
(excluding pointed edging)

45cm/17¾ in for all sizes

MATERIALS

- 13(15:17) 50g balls of Debbie Bliss alpaca silk dk in Chocolate 13.
- Set of four 4mm (US 6) double pointed knitting needles.
- Short and long 4mm (US 6) circular knitting needles.
- 3.00mm (US size D) crochet hook (optional).
- Decorative pin to fasten.

TENSION

22 sts and 28 rows to 10cm/4in square over st st using 4mm (US 6) needles.

ABBREVIATIONS

See page 7.

NOTES

- The back and fronts are worked in the round in one circular piece, starting at the centre, with gaps left for the armholes. The sleeves are picked up and worked down to the cuff.
- The crochet hook is used only for the centre cast on. If you prefer, just cast on the stitches in the usual way.
- You'll need double pointed needles to work the centre of the cardigan, change to the short, then the long circular needle when there are too many stitches to work comfortably on the double pointed needles.
- Use the shorter circular needle to pick up the sleeve stitches, changing to double pointed needles when convenient.
- Use a point protector or wind a rubber band around the tip of the first needle to mark the start of the rounds. When you transfer to a circular needle, use a plastic ring or a loop of contrast thread as a marker.

BACK AND FRONTS

With 3.00mm (US size D) crochet hook, make 5 chain, slip stitch in first chain to form a ring. Make 1 chain for first st, * insert hook in ring, yarn around hook and pull through ring, yarn around hook and pull through first loop on hook to make 2nd st, place these 2 sts on first needle; rep from * until 8 sts have been made, placing next 2 sts on 2nd needle and last 4 sts on 3rd needle.
If casting on using double pointed needles and not the crochet hook, just cast on 8 sts and place the sts on 3 needles as given above, being careful not to twist the cast on edge.
Join in a ring.
1st round (right side) K.
Inc round [K1, yo] to end. 16 sts.
K 3 rounds.
Work inc round again. 32 sts.
K 5 rounds.
Work inc round again. 64 sts.
K 7 rounds.
Work inc round again. 128 sts.
K 9(12:14) rounds.
Work inc round again. 256 sts.
K 11(15:19) rounds.
Work inc round again. 512 sts.
K 13(18:23) rounds.
1st size only
Eyelet round [K2tog, yo] to end.

2nd and 3rd sizes only
Inc round * [K2tog, yo] (31:15) times, [k1, yo] twice, rep from
* (7:15) more times.
All sizes
512(528:544) sts.
K 6(9:12) rounds.
Shape armholes
1st round K58, cast off 48(52:56) sts, with one st on right
needle after cast off, k until there are 300(308:316) sts after
left armhole, cast off 48(52:56) sts, with one st on right needle
after cast off, k until there are 58 sts after right armhole.
2nd round K58, cast on 48(52:56) sts, k300(308:316), cast
on 48(52:56) sts, k58. 512(528:544) sts.
K 7(10:13) rounds.
1st size only
Next round [K2tog, yo] 256 times.
2nd and 3rd sizes only
Next round * [K2tog, yo] (16:8) times, k(1:1), yo, rep from *
(15:31) more times.
All sizes
512(544:576) sts.
K 17(21:25) rounds.
Eyelet round [K2tog, yo] to end.
K 19(23:26) rounds.
Now work lacy patt as follows:
1st round [K2tog, yo] to end.
2nd round K.
3rd round [Yo, skpo] to end.
4th round K.
These 4 rounds form the lacy patt.
Work 8(12:16) more rounds in lacy patt.
P 1 round.
Now work pointed edging as follows:
1st row K1, turn.
2nd row K1.
3rd row K2, turn.
4th row K2.
5th row K3, turn.
6th row K3.
7th row K4, turn.
8th row K4.
9th row K5, turn.
10th row K5.
11th row K6, turn.
12th row K6.
13th row K7, turn.
14th row K 7.
15th row K8, turn.
16th row K8.
17th row Cast off 8 sts, with one st on right needle, turn.
2nd to 17th rows form the patt and are repeated.
Cont in patt until 16th row of 64th(68th:72nd) point has been
completed.
Next row Cast off 7 sts, pick up one st from first st of round,
cast off one st.
Fasten off.

SLEEVES

With right side facing, beg at underarm, pick up and k
48(52:56) sts up first side of armhole, 2 sts from row-ends at
top of armhole and 48(52:56) sts down 2nd side of armhole
98(106:114) sts.
K 1 round.
Eyelet round [K2tog, yo] to end.
K 1 round.
Dec round (right side) K1, k2tog, k to last 3 sts, skpo, k1.
96(104:112) sts.
Cont to k every round for st st and dec in this way on
10 foll alt rounds, then on 14 foll 7th rounds. 48(56:64) sts.
K 1 round.
Work 6 rounds in lacy patt as given for Back/Fronts.
Work pointed edging as given for Back/Fronts, finishing
with 6th(7th:8th) point with final 17th row.
Fasten off.

TO MAKE UP

Press lightly according to ball band. Pin at front to fasten.

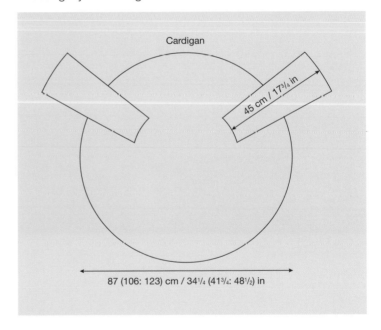

Cardigan

45 cm / 17¾ in

87 (106: 123) cm / 34¼ (41¾: 48½) in

Smocked Cables Jacket

MEASUREMENTS

To fit bust

81–86	91–97	102–107	cm
32–34	36–38	40–42	in

FINISHED MEASUREMENTS

Bust

105	115	125	cm
41½	45¼	49¼	in

Length

58	59	61	cm
22¾	23¼	24	in

Sleeve length

47cm/18½in for all sizes

MATERIALS

- 18(19:20) 50g hanks of Debbie Bliss SoHo in Lagoon 19.
- Pair each 4½mm (US 7) and 5½ mm (US 9) knitting needles.
- Cable needle.
- 45(50:50)cm/18(20:20)in open-ended zip.

TENSION

16 sts and 22 rows to 10cm/4in square over st st using 5½ mm (US 9) needles.

ABBREVIATIONS

C4B = slip next 2 sts onto cable needle, hold at back of work, k2, then k2 from cable needle.
C4F = slip next 2 sts onto cable needle, hold at front of work, k2, then k2 from cable needle.
C3BP = slip next st onto cable needle, hold at back of work, k2, then p1 from cable needle.
C3FP = slip next 2 sts onto cable needle, hold at front of work, p1, then k2 from cable needle.
kfb = k into front and back of st.
pfb = p into front and back of st.
wrap 4 = slip next 4 sts onto cable needle, take yarn behind and three times around 4 sts on cable needle, then k the 4 sts.
Also see page 7.

NOTE

Front is 2 rows longer than back to match the pattern on the shoulders.

PATT PANEL (Worked over 26 sts)

1st row (right side) P3, [wrap 4, p4] twice, wrap 4, p3.
2nd and every wrong side row K and p the sts as they appear.
3rd row P2, [C3BP, C3FP, p2] 3 times.
5th row P2, k2, p2, [C3FP, C3BP, p2] twice, k2, p2.
7th row P2, k2, p3, wrap 4, p4, wrap 4, p3, k2, p2.
9th row P2, k2, p2, [C3BP, C3FP, p2] twice, k2, p2.
11th row P2, [C3FP, C3BP, p2] 3 times.
12th row See 2nd row.
These 12 rows form the Smocked Cable Patt Panel.

BACK

With 4½ mm (US 7) needles, cast on 102(110:118) sts.
1st row (right side) K2, [p2, k2] to end.
2nd row P2, [k2, p2] to end.
These 2 rows form rib.
Rib 18 more rows.
Change to 5½ mm (US 9) needles.
Dec row (right side) K6(10:14), * p2, k1, skpo, k2tog, k1, p2, [C3F, C3B, p2] 3 times, k1, skpo, k2tog, k1, p2 *, k6; rep from * to *, k6(10:14). 94(102:110) sts.

Next row K and p the sts as they appear.

These 2 rows **set** the position for cable panels and **form** st st at each side and between panels.

Now work in patt as follows:

1st row (right side) K6(10:14), * p2, C4B, patt 26 sts of 1st row of Patt Panel, C4F, p2 *, k6, rep from * to *, k6(10:14).

2nd and every wrong side row K and p the sts as they appear.

3rd row K6(10:14), * p2, k4, work 26 sts of 3rd row of Patt Panel, k4, p2 *, k6, rep from * to *, k6(10:14).

4th row As 2nd row.

These 4 rows **form** the rope cables at each side of panels. Working correct Patt Panel rows, cont in patt and work 10 rows.

Inc row (right side) K2, kfb, patt to last 4 sts, kfb, k3. 96(104:112) sts.

Cont in patt, inc in this way at each end of 5 foll 6th rows. 106(114:122) sts.

Patt 19 rows.

Shape armholes

Cast off 6 sts at beg of next 2 rows. 94(102:110) sts.

Dec row (right side) Skpo, patt to last 2 sts, k2tog. 92(100:108) sts.

Dec in this way at each end of next 6(7:8) right side rows. 80(86:92) sts.

Patt 29(31:33) rows.

Cast off.

Place markers 19(22:25) sts in from each end of cast off row.

LEFT FRONT

With 4½ mm (US 7) needles, cast on 51(55:59) sts.

1st row (right side) K2, [p2, k2] to last st, k1.

2nd row P3, [k2, p2] to end.

These 2 rows form rib with one extra st at front edge.

Work 18 more rows.

Change to 5½ mm (US 9) needles.

Dec row (right side) K6(10:14), p2, k1, skpo, k2tog, k1, p2, [C3F, C3B, p2] 3 times, k1, skpo, k2tog, k1, p2, k3. 47(51:55) sts.

Next row K and p the sts as they appear.

These 2 rows **set** the position for the Patt Panel and **form** st st at each side.

Now work in patt as follows:

1st row (right side) K6(10:14), p2, C4B, patt 26 sts of 1st row of Patt Panel, C4F, p2, k3.

2nd and every wrong side row K and p the sts as they appear.

3rd row K6(10:14), p2, k4, work 26 sts of 3rd row of Patt Panel, k4, p2, k3.

4th row As 2nd row.

These 4 rows **form** cables at each side of panels. Working correct patt panel rows, cont in patt and work 10 rows.

Inc row (right side) K2, kfb, patt to end. 48(52:56) sts.

Cont in patt, inc in this way at beg of 5 foll 6th rows.

53(57:61) sts.

Patt 19 rows.

Shape armhole

Cast off 6 sts at beg of next row. 47(51:55) sts.

Patt 1 row.

Dec row (right side) Skpo, patt to end. 46(50:54) sts.

Dec in this way at beg of next 6(7:8) right side rows. 40(43:46) sts.

Patt 9(11:13) rows.

Shape neck

1st row (right side) Patt 37(40:43) sts, turn and leave 3 sts on a holder for neck.

Dec one st at neck edge on next 9 rows. 28(31:34) sts.

Patt one row.

Dec one st at neck edge on next 3 rows. 25(28:31) sts.

Work last 4 rows twice more. 19(22:25) sts.

Cast off.

RIGHT FRONT

With 4½ mm (US 7) needles, cast on 51(55:59) sts.

1st row (right side) K3, [p2, k2] to end.

2nd row [P2, k2] to last 3 sts, p3.

These 2 rows form rib with one extra st at front edge.

Work 18 more rows.

Change to 5½ mm (US 9) needles.

Dec row (right side) K3, p2, k1, skpo, k2tog, k1, p2, [C3F, C3B, p2] 3 times, k1, skpo, k2tog, k1, p2, k6(10:14). 47(51:55) sts.

Next row K and p the sts as they appear.

These 2 rows **set** the position for the Patt Panel and **form** st st at each side.

Now work in patt as follows:

1st row (right side) K3, p2, C4B, patt 26 sts of 1st row of Patt Panel, C4F, p2, k6(10:14).

2nd and every wrong side row K and p the sts as they appear.

3rd row K3, p2, k4, work 26 sts of 3rd row of Patt Panel, k4, p2, k6(10:14).

4th row As 2nd row.

These 4 rows **form** rope cables at each side of panels. Working correct Patt Panel rows, cont in patt and work 10 rows.

Inc row (right side) Patt to last 4 sts, kfb, k3. 48(52:56) sts.

Cont in patt, inc in this way at end of 5 foll 6th rows. 53(57:61) sts.

Patt 20 rows.

Shape armhole

Cast off 6 sts at beg of next row. 47(51:55) sts.

Dec row (right side) Patt to last 2 sts, k2tog. 46(50:54) sts.

Dec in this way at end of next 6(7:8) right side rows. 40(43:46) sts.

Patt 9(11:13) rows.

Shape neck

1st row (right side) K3 and leave these 3 sts on a holder for neck, patt to end. 37(40:43) sts.

Dec one st at neck edge on next 9 rows. 28(31:34) sts.
Patt one row.
Dec one st at neck edge on next 3 rows. 25(28:31) sts.
Work last 4 rows twice more. 19(22:25) sts.
Cast off.

SLEEVES

With 4½ mm (US 7) needles, cast on 54 sts.
Work 20 rows in rib as given for Back.
Change to 5½ mm (US 9) needles.
Dec row (right side) K6, p2, k1, skpo, k2tog, k1, p2,
[C3F, C3B, p2] 3 times, k1, skpo, k2tog, k1, p2, k6. 50 sts.
Next row K and p the sts as they appear.
These 2 rows **set** the position for the Patt Panel and **form**
st st at each side.
Now work in patt as follows:
1st row (right side) K6, p2, C4B, patt 26 sts of 1st row
of Patt Panel, C4F, p2, k6.
2nd and every wrong side row K and p the sts as they
appear.
3rd row K6, p2, k4, work 26 sts of 3rd row of Patt Panel,
k4, p2, k6.
4th row As 2nd row.
These 4 rows **form** rope cables at each side of panels.
Cont in patt and work 2 rows.
Inc row (right side) K2, kfb, patt to last 4 sts, kfb, k3. 52 sts.
Cont in patt, inc in this way at each end of 9(12:15) foll
8th(6th:4th) rows. 70(76:82) sts.
Patt 7(7:19) rows.
Shape top
Cast off 6 sts at beg of next 2 rows. 58(64:70) sts.
Dec row (right side) Skpo, patt to last 2 sts, k2tog.
56(62:68) sts.
Dec in this way at each end of next 6(7:8) right side rows.
44(48:52) sts.
Patt 5 rows without shaping.
Dec in same way as before at each end of next row
and on next 4(5:6) right side rows. 34(36:38) sts.
Patt 1 row.
Cast off.

FRONT EDGES

With 4½ mm (US 7) needles, pick up and k 75(78:81) sts
along right front edge.
Cast off knitwise.
Work left front edge in the same way.

COLLAR

Join shoulder seams, using back edge markers as a guide.
Right side of collar
With 5½ mm (US 9) needles, slip 3 sts from right front
holder onto needle.
1st row (wrong side of work, right side of collar) K3
2nd row K2, kfb. 4 sts.

3rd row K4.
4th row K3, pfb. 5 sts.
5th row K5.
6th row K3, p1, pfb. 6 sts.
7th row K6.
8th row K3, p2, pfb. 7 sts.
9th row K7.
10th row K3, p3, pfb. 8 sts.
11th row P1, C4F, k3.
12th row K3, p4, kfb. 9 sts.
13th row P2, k7.
14th row K3, p4, k1, kfb. 10 sts.
15th row K1, p2, C4F, k3.
16th row K3, p4, k2, pfb. 11 sts.
17th row K2, p2, k7.
Working k3 border and 4-st rope cable as set, cont increasing
at neck edge on every right side row until there are 19 sts,
taking inc sts into k2, p2 rib.
Leave sts on a holder.
Left side of collar
With 5½ mm (US 9) needles and with right side facing,
k3 from holder.
Inc one st at end of next and every collar right side row,
taking inc sts into C4B cable, then into k2, p2 rib until
there are 19 sts.
Work 1 row.
Joining row (right side of collar) Patt 19 sts of left side of
collar, pick up and k 42 sts across back neck, patt 19 sts
of right side of collar. 80 sts.
Patt 24 rows.
K 4 rows.
Cast off knitwise.

ZIP END COVERS (make 2)

With 4½ mm (US 7) needles, cast on 3 sts and work
3 rows in st st.
Cast off.

TO MAKE UP

Join shaped edge of collar to front neck edges. Sew in zip.
If zip is too long, fold top ends back, secure and trim.
Sew zip end covers over top of zip ends. Sew sleeves into
armholes. Join side and sleeve seams.

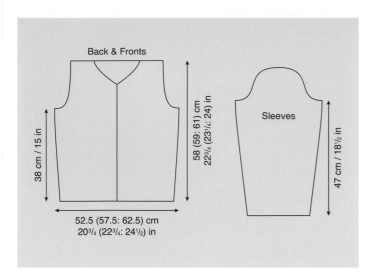

Back & Fronts

38 cm / 15 in

58 (59: 61) cm
22¾ (23¼: 24) in

52.5 (57.5: 62.5) cm
20¾ (22¾: 24½) in

Sleeves

47 cm / 18½ in

Shaped Edge Sweater

MEASUREMENTS

To fit bust

81–86	92–97	102–107	112–117	cm
32–34	36–38	40–42	44–46	in

FINISHED MEASUREMENTS

Bust

101	109	116	123	cm
39¾	43	45½	48½	in

Length at centre front

53	57	61	65	cm
20¾	22½	24	25½	in

Sleeve length

46cm/18in for all sizes.

MATERIALS

- 14(15:16:17) 50g balls of Debbie Bliss cashmerino aran in Teal 10.
- Pair 5mm (US 8) knitting needles.
- Short 4½mm (US 7) and 5mm (US 8) circular knitting needles.

TENSIONS

24 sts and 26 rows to 10cm/4in over rib when slightly stretched, using 5mm (US 8) needles.
Work a tension square over k1, p1 rib and measure this to obtain the correct tension, the width of the garment is calculated over a different tension as the rib at this point is diagonal, and the central 2 sts have a row tension of 23 rows to 10cm/4in.

ABBREVIATIONS

m1p = make one st purlwise by picking up and purling into back of loop lying between st just worked and next st.
ssk = sl 1 knitwise, sl 1 knitwise, insert point of left hand needle from back to front through these 2 slipped sts and k them tog.
Also see page 7.

NOTES

- Back and front length measurements are taken along the central line.
- All seams should be joined, working from the right side in mattress st, working into the centre of the edge st, so forming a complete knit st when joined.

BACK AND FRONT (both alike)

With 5mm (US 8) needles, cast on 114(122:130:138) sts
1st foundation row [K1, p1] 28(30:32:34) times, k2, [p1, k1] 28(30:32:34) times.
Now work in patt as follows:
1st row (wrong side) [P1, k1] 28(30:32:34) times, p2, [k1, p1] 28(30:32:34) times.
2nd row K1, m1, [p1, k1] 27(29:31:33) times, k2tog, ssk, [k1, p1] 27(29:31:33), m1, k1.
3rd row P2, [k1, p1] 27(29:31:33) times, p2, [p1, k1] 27(29:31:33) times, p2.
4th row K1, m1p, [k1, p1] 27(29:31:33) times, k2tog, ssk, [p1, k1] 27(29:31:33) times, m1p, k1.
These 4 rows form the patt and are repeated.
Cont in patt until work measures 31(33:35:37)cm/12¼(13:13¼:14½)in from cast on edge, when measured along the centre line, ending with a 1st patt row.
Shape armholes
Next row (right side) Cast off 4 sts, with one st on needle after cast off, work [p1, k1] 25(27:29:31) times, k2tog, ssk, [k1, p1] 27(29:31:33) times, k1.
Next row Cast off 4 sts, with one st on needle after cast off, work [k1, p1] 24(26:28:30) times, k1, p4, [k1, p1] 25(27:29:31) times. 104(112:120:128) sts.
Keeping patt correct, cont to work decs at centre front, but do not work incs at side edges.
Cont until 54(58:62:66) sts rem, ending with a right side row.
Next row [P1, k1] 1(2:3:1) times, [p3tog, k1, p1, k1] 4(4:4:5) times, p2tog, [k1, p1, k1, p3tog] 4(4:4:5) times, [k1, p1]

1(2:3:1) times.
Leave rem 37(41:45:45) sts on a holder.

SLEEVES

With 5mm (US 8) needles, cast on 66(70:74:78) sts.
1st row [K1, p1] 16(17:18:19) times, k2, [p1, k1] 16(17:18:19) times.
2nd row [P1, k1] 16(17:18:19) times, p2, [k1, p1] 16(17:18:19) times.
3rd row As 1st row.
4th row As 2nd row.
5th row K1, m1, [p1, k1] 15(16:17:18) times, k2tog, ssk, [k1, p1] 15(16:17:18) times, m1, k1.
6th row P2, [k1, p1] 15(16:17:18) times, p2, [p1, k1] 15(16:17:18) times, p2.
7th row K2, [p1, k1] 15(16:17:18) times, k2, [k1, p1] 15(16:17:18), k2.
8th row As 6th row.
9th row (1st inc row) K1, m1p, [k1, p1] 15(16:17:18) times, k4, [p1, k1] 15(16:17:18) times, m1p, k1. 68(72:76:80) sts.
10th row [P1, k1] 16(17:18:19) times, p4, [k1, p1] 16(17:18:19) times.
11th row [K1, p1] 16(17:18:19) times, k4, [p1, k1] 16(17:18:19) times.
12th row As 10th row.
13th row K1, m1, [p1, k1] 15(16:17:18) times, p1, k2tog, ssk, p1, [k1, p1] 15(16:17:18) times, m1, k1.
14th row P2, [k1, p1] 15(16:17:18) times, k1, p2, k1, [p1, k1] 15(16:17:18) times, p2.
15th row K2, [p1, k1] 15(16:17:18) times, p1, k2, p1, [k1, p1] 15(16:17:18), k2.
16th row As 14th row.
17th row (2nd inc row) K1, m1p, [k1, p1] 16(17:18:19) times, k2, [p1, k1] 16(17:18:19) times, m1p, k1. 70(74:78:82) sts.
18th row [P1, k1] 17(18:19:20) times, p2, [k1, p1] 17(18:19:20) times.
19th row [K1, p1] 17(18:19:20) times, k2, [p1, k1] 17(18:19:20) times.
20th row As 18th row.
21st row K1, m1, [p1, k1] 16(17:18:19) times, k2tog, ssk, [k1, p1] 16(17:18:19) times, m1, k1.
Cont in this way, increasing 1 st at each end of every 4th row and decreasing 2 sts at centre of every 8th row, until 14 central double decs and 28 side edge incs have been worked, ending with a side inc row. 94(98:102:106) sts.
Patt 1 row without shaping.
Shape armholes
** Cast off 4 sts at beg of next 2 rows. 86(90:94:98) sts.
Next row (right side) Patt 41(43:45:47) sts, k2tog, ssk, patt 41(43:45:47). 84(88:92:96) sts.
Next row K all k sts and p all p sts as they appear.
Next row Patt 40(42:44:46) sts, k2tog, ssk, patt 40(42:44:46). 82(86:90:94) sts.
Next row K all k sts and p all p sts as they appear.
Cont in rib and dec 2 sts in this way at centre of every

foll right side row until 38 sts rem, ending with a right side row.
Patt 2 rows without central decreases.
[51(55:59:63) rows have been worked from **]
Next row (wrong side) [P1, k1, p3tog, k1] 3 times, p2tog, [k1, p3tog, k1] 3 times.
Leave rem 25 sts on a holder.

COLLAR

With right side facing and 4½mm (US 7) circular needle, starting at left sleeve, work as follows: sl 1, [p1, k1] 11 times, p1, k last st of left sleeve tog with first st of front, [p1, k1] 17(19:21:21) times, p1, k last st tog with first st of right sleeve, [p1, k1] 11 times, p1, k last st of right sleeve tog with first st of back, [p1, k1] 17(19:21:21) times, p1, k last st tog with first slipped st of left sleeve. 120(128:136:136) sts.
Place a marker to indicate the beg of the round.
Every round [K1, p1] 60(64:68:68) times.
Work in rounds of rib until collar measures 9cm/3½ in.
Change to 5mm (US 8) circular needle and cont in rib rounds for a further 9cm/3½ in.
Cast off loosely but evenly in rib.

TO MAKE UP

See Notes for joining seams, then join raglan seams, side seams and sleeve seams.

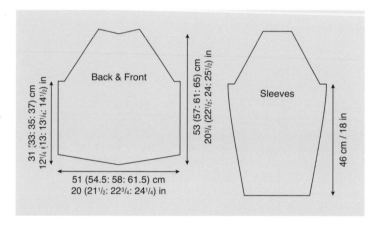

Back & Front

31 (33: 35: 37) cm
12¼ (13: 13¾: 14½) in

53 (57: 61: 65) cm
20¾ (22½: 24: 25½) in

51 (54.5: 58: 61.5) cm
20 (21½: 22¾: 24¼) in

Sleeves

46 cm / 18 in

Distributors

For stockists of Debbie Bliss yarns please contact:

UK

Designer Yarns Ltd
Units 8-10 Newbridge Industrial Estate
Pitt Street, Keighley
W. Yorkshire BD21 4PQ
UK

T: +44 (0)1535 664222
F: +44 (0)1535 664333
E: david@designeryarns.uk.com
www.designeryarns.uk.com

USA

Knitting Fever Inc.
315 Bayview Avenue
Amityville
NY 11701
USA

T: 001 516 546 3600
F: 001 516 546 6871
www.knittingfever.com

CANADA

Diamond Yarns Ltd
155 Martin Ross Avenue Unit 3
Toronto
Ontario M3J 2L9
CANADA

T: 001 416 736 6111
F: 001 416 736 6112
www.diamondyarn.com

MEXICO

Estambres Crochet SA de CV
Aaron Saenz 1891-7
Col. Santa Maria
Monterrey
N.L. 64650
MEXICO

T: (52) 81 8335 3870
E: abremer@redmundial.com.mx

BELGIUM/HOLLAND

Pavan
Meerlaanstraat 73
9860 Balegem (Oostrezele)
BELGIUM

T: +32 (0) 9 221 85 94
F: +32 (0) 9 221 56 62
E: pavan@pandora.be

ICELAND

Storkurinn
Langavegi 59
101 Reykjavík
ICELAND

T: +354 551 8258
F: +354 562 8252

GERMANY/AUSTRIA/SWITZERLAND

Designer Yarns
Handelsagentur Klaus Koch
Sachsstrasse 30
D-50259 Pulheim-Brauweiler
GERMANY

T: +49 (0) 2234 205453
F: +49 (0) 2234 205456
E: kk@designeryarns.de
www.designeryarns.de

FRANCE

Elle Tricote
8 Rue du Coq, La Petite France
67000 Strasbourg
FRANCE

T: +33 (0) 388 230313
F: +33 (0) 8823 0169
www.elletricote.com

SPAIN

Oyambre
Pau Claris 145
08009 Barcelona
SPAIN

T: +34 934 87 2672
F: +34 67870 8614
E: marian@oyambreonline.com

SWEDEN/DENMARK/NORWAY

Hamilton Design
Storgatan 14
SE-64730 Mariefred
SWEDEN

T: +46 (0)159 12006
F: +46 (0) 159 21805
www.hamiltondesign.biz

AUSTRALIA

Prestige Yarns Pty Ltd
P O Box 39
Bulli NSW 2516
AUSTRALIA

T: +61 02 4285 6669
E: info@prestigeyarns.com
www.prestigeyarns.com

FINLAND

Vilmiinan Villapouti
Näsilinnankatu 23
33210 Tampere
FINLAND

T/F: +358 (0)3 2129676
E: info@villapouti.net

JAPAN

Hobbyra Hobbyre
5-23-37 Higashi-Ohi
Shinagawa-ku
Tokyo 140-0011
JAPAN

T: (81) 3 3472 1104
F: (81) 3 3472 1196

For more information on my other yarns and books, please visit www.debbieblissonline.com